Advance Praise for
Understanding Arabs

For 15 years, Margaret Nydell's *Understanding Arabs* has been used by countless Americans preparing to work or live in the Arab World. It is a unique source; there is nothing like it. Written with wit as well as seriousness, it provides a sound cultural appreciation as well as basic data on the region. A new appendix, "Muslims and Arabs in the West," constitutes a major innovation in the third edition. But her personal message regarding the tragic events of September 11 should be required reading by all who make decisions or write commentary on the Arab world.

—Max L. Gross
Joint Military Intelligence College

This is an important and fascinating book, especially for Americans in this crucial time in U.S.-Arab relations. Dr. Nydell presents a timely, lucid, and engaging guide to the values and cultures of the Arab World, based on her many years of working and living there and on her training as a professional linguist. This candid and wonderfully readable book captures the contrasts and the characteristics of this great civilization and brings them vividly to life for a Western audience.

—Karin Ryding, Ph.D.
Sultan Qaboos bin Said Professor of Arabic
Chair of the Department of Arabic Language
Georgetown University

Ever wonder what the Arabs are thinking? *Understanding Arabs* offers both an analysis and a perspective that are in great demand. This book covers what the media typically overlook and what is *necessary* to make some sense of what is going on. We have relied on this source of cultural information for many years. I have found no other book in English to be so useful.

—Colonel Terrence M. Potter, US Military Academy

Middle East specialists have long relied on their worn copies of *Understanding Arabs* for insights about Arab social behavior. Following September 11, a third edition of this classic could not be more timely. A whole generation of U.S. diplomats were introduced to the subject by Dr. Nydell...in the 1970s and 1980s. In this concise and practical guide, she shares her wealth of scholarly and real-world experience, and she does so without the psycho-babble that too often dominates other surveys of the subject.

—Ambassador David L. Mack, Vice President
Middle East Institute, Washington, D.C.

Among other things the events of September 11 dramatized our ignorance as Americans about Arabs and Islam. This book helps to fill that void by exploring the enormous misconceptions we hold about each other. In this work...Nydell explores both the background and context for our mutual misunderstandings. She discusses beliefs and values, relationships between men and women, etiquette and social structure, communication styles, religion, the Arabic language, and both the similarities and differences among the various Arab nations. As a result, we not only recognize the basis for misunderstanding but also the need for increased information and communication.... A must book for all!

—Alvino E. Fantini, Former President, SIETAR International
Senior Faculty, School for International Training
Brattleboro, Vermont

Understanding
Arabs

The InterAct Series

Other books in the series:

AU CONTRAIRE! FIGURING OUT THE FRENCH
BORDER CROSSINGS: AMERICAN INTERACTIONS WITH ISRAELIS
ENCOUNTERING THE CHINESE
EXPLORING THE GREEK MOSAIC
A FAIR GO FOR ALL: AUSTRALIAN/AMERICAN INTERACTIONS
FROM DA TO YES: UNDERSTANDING THE EAST EUROPEANS
FROM NYET TO DA: UNDERSTANDING THE RUSSIANS
GERMANY: UNRAVELING AN ENIGMA
GOOD NEIGHBORS: COMMUNICATING WITH THE MEXICANS
INTO AFRICA
LEARNING TO THINK KOREAN
MODERN-DAY VIKINGS
SPAIN IS DIFFERENT
WITH RESPECT TO THE JAPANESE

Understanding
Arabs
A Guide for Westerners

Third Edition

Margaret K. (Omar) Nydell

INTERCULTURAL PRESS, INC.

First published by Intercultural Press. For information, contact:

Intercultural Press, Inc.
PO Box 700
Yarmouth, Maine 04096 USA
Tel: 207-846-5168
Fax: 207-846-5181
www.interculturalpress.com

Nicholas Brealey Publishing
3–5 Spafield Street
London EC1R 4QB, UK
Tel: +44-207-239-0360
Fax: +44-207-239-0370
www.nbrealey-books.com

Book design and production by Patty J. Topel
Cover design and production by Patty J. Topel

Printed in the United States of America

06   05   04   03   2   3   4   5

Library of Congress Cataloging-in-Publication Data

Nydell, Margaret K. (Margaret Kleffner)
    Understanding Arabs : a guide for Westerners / Margaret K. (Omar) Nydell.—3rd. ed.
       p. cm.—(The InterAct series)
       Includes bibliographical references.
       ISBN 1-877864-15-3
       1. Arabs. I. Title. II. Series.
DS36.77.N93 2002
909'.04927—dc21   2002068589

Contents

A Message from the Author ix
Map of the Arab World xvii
Preface xix

Introduction: Patterns of Change 1
      Modernization 1
      The Effects of Change 6
      The Muslim View 9
      Fundamentalism (Islamism) 15
      Facing the Future 21

1   Beliefs and Values 23
      Basic Arab Values 25
      Basic Arab Religious Attitudes 25
      Basic Arab Self-Perceptions 26

2   Friends and Strangers 29
      The Concept of Friendship 29
      Reciprocal Favors 30
      Introductions 32
      Visiting Patterns 33
      Business Friendships 35
      Office Relations 36

Criticism   37
Intermediaries   39
Private and Public Manners   40

3   Emotion and Logic 43
Objectivitiy and Subjectivity   43
Fatalism   44
What Is Reality?   45
The Human Dimension   47
Persuasion 48

4   Getting Personal 51
Personal Questions   51
Sensitive Subjects   52
Social Distance   54
Gestures   56
Names   57

5   Men and Women 63
Social Interaction 63
Displaying Intimacy   65
The Status of Women   65
Western Women   68

6   Social Formalities and Etiquette 71
Hospitality   71
Time and Appointments   74
Discussing Business   75
Sharing Meals   76
Smoking   80
Rules of Etiquette   80

7   The Social Structure 85
Social Classes   85
Image and Upper-Class Behavior   86
Dealing with Service People   88

8 The Role of the Family 91
   Family Loyalty and Obligations 91
   Relations among Family Members 93
   Marriage 95
   Divorce 96
   Child-Rearing Practices 97
   Talking about Your Family 100

9 Religion and Society 101
   Religious Affiliation 101
   Religious Practices 101
   The Religion of Islam 103
   The Qur'an and the Bible 108
   Passages from the Qur'an 111

10 Communicating with Arabs 115
   Varieties of Arabic 116
   The Superiority of Arabic 117
   The Prestige of Classical Arabic 118
   Eloquence of Speech 119
   Speech Mannerisms 120
   The Power of Words 122
   Euphemisms 123
   The Written Word 124
   Proverbs 124

Conclusion 127

Appendix A. Muslims and Arabs in the West 129
   Muslims in the United States and Canada 129
   Arabs in the United States 131
   Muslims in Europe 132
   Arabs in Western Europe 135
   Image in the West 136
   Image in America 136
   Image in Europe 140

Islamic Schools   144
Headscarves   144

Appendix B. The Arab Countries: Similarities
   and Differences 147
      Morocco   148
      Algeria   151
      Tunisia   153
      Libya   155
      Egypt   157
      Sudan   160
      Lebanon   162
      Syria   164
      Jordan   166
      Iraq   168
      Saudi Arabia   170
      Yemen   174
      Kuwait   177
      The Arabian Gulf States   178

Appendix C. The Arabic Language 185
      Colloquial Arabic Dialects   186
      Attitudes toward Dialects   188
      The Structure of Arabic   188
      Arabic Writing   190
      Calligraphy as an Art Form   191
      Social Greetings   192

Bibliography and References 195

About the Author 217

A Message from the Author

In the late morning of 11 September 2001, I walked from the Georgetown University campus in Washington, D.C., and crossed the Key Bridge into Virginia. I found many buildings evacuated, public transportation stopped, and all roads going past the Pentagon blocked off. I finally found a taxi, and the driver assured me that he would help me get home to Crystal City by skirting around the Pentagon area and going far into Virginia. He did so, brilliantly, using small residential streets, until I was close enough to walk home. It took over an hour. He was Pakistani and, of course, Muslim. He was near tears (I was crying openly). He did not want to take any money. He said he was going to do this all day as a public service. I gave him money anyway and told him that if he didn't want to take it, he could donate it to Zakat charity (Islamic alms).

The shock of Black Tuesday brought all Americans together in a moment of clarity—we are one nation. I hope this clarity will persist and will encourage us to seek greater understanding of other cultures. America is part of the world. We are all one family now. We are all in it together.

The terrorist attacks on the World Trade Center and the Pentagon on 11 September left Americans and millions of others around the world bewildered as well as shocked and angry. Who could have committed such an atrocity? As the smoke cleared, a Saudi Arab, Osama Bin Laden, became identified as the chief perpetrator, commanding a network called Al Qaeda, which was unknown a few years ago. Its known members and accomplices are mostly Arabs and are all Muslims.*

People all over the world are asking why. Why the United States? What could have motivated this act? The media, impelled as always to provide instant answers, came up with a variety of theories of varying degrees of merit. Some of them were based on popular misconceptions about Muslims, notably:

＊ This is a religion- and culture-based clash—the "clash of civilizations" theory. The Bin Laden group is characterized as representative of the thinking of the majority of Muslims.

＊ The attackers (and others who "hate America") are envious of the American "way of life." They want to change American values and eliminate American freedoms.

＊ These particular attackers were motivated by visions of rewards in Paradise because for them this was a Jihad (a so-called Holy War) against unbelievers.

---

* Al Qaeda arose from a puritanical version of Islam, Wahhabism, which is followed officially only in Saudi Arabia. It has become the prevailing interpretation of Islam among the Taliban group. The Wahhabi version of Islam forbids, for example, theaters and churches. It forbids the marking of graves. No alcohol or pork products may be imported. Publications are censored. Government-appointed officials enforce the law that requires all commercial establishments to close during prayer time. Wahhabis require women to cover their faces. Other Muslim countries generally do not follow these rules.

All of these explanations are without merit. They do not conform to the facts. They confuse the motives of this particular terrorist group with the prevailing discontent in the Islamic world. But the Al Qaeda group did not come out of nothing; it is an aberrant, cultlike faction that grew out of the Mideast milieu. This terrorist act, although rooted in political grievances, was an expression of the group's anger, through terrorist violence, for its own sake.

Statements such as "They hate American freedom" and "They want to destroy America" do not satisfy for long—they are impossibly vague. As time passes, people will begin to identify reasons that make more sense. They will dig deeper, because unless the terrorists are all crazy or all evil, there must be better reasons. If the three statements above were true, they would lead us first to despair, then to defiance, and ultimately back to despair.

Perhaps the reasons include things we don't understand or even know about. For example, resentments against the United States in particular have grown out of a context with which few Americans are familiar. The resentments are not primarily against American wealth and power as such. Rather, they reflect profound dismay at how America is perceived to *use* its unique wealth and power when dealing with other countries and cultures.

Perceptions become realities to the people who hold them, and people who lack cross-cultural experience can easily misunderstand the attitudes and behaviors they confront. Americans, for example, are notoriously ill-informed about the Mideast. In turn, the average Mideastern individual may be keenly interested in American political policies but actually knows very little about Western societies. Each side has enormous misconceptions about the other.

Language is a huge barrier. If we accept the premise that all people express themselves more accurately and candidly in their own language, then we should be skeptical about statements being reported from conversations with foreigners, filtered through English or other languages. Unfortunately, too many of our Mideast experts and reporters do not speak the local languages (imagine an expert on the U.S. who did not speak English). Thus they have severely limited access to information, and they may gravitate toward people with whom they can communicate easily, people who sometimes misrepresent the thinking of the general populace.

There are many arguments that can be made on both sides, but one thing is certain: the language barrier accounts for much of the misunderstanding on both sides. In the thirty-five years I have been listening to political discussions in Arabic, among Arabs who were talking to one another and not to me, I have never heard resentment expressed about anything American except for foreign policy. Mideasterners in general care only about American activities that negatively affect their own lives.

Consider the explanations offered by the terrorist leaders and others we have associated with terrorist movements. We must not ignore what they are saying; we must try to understand their statements, recognizing that this does not require agreeing with them.

* Bin Laden: "They violate our land and occupy it and steal the Muslims' possessions, and when faced with resistance, they call it terrorism.... What America is tasting now is something insignificant compared with what we have tasted for scores of years. Our nation has been tasting this humiliation and this degradation for more than eighty years."

* Muhammad Omar, leader of the Taliban: "America has created the evil that is attacking it...the U.S. should step back and review its policy."

* A spokesman, Muslim Brotherhood (Egypt): "We want to understand, are you Americans in favor of human rights and freedom? Or is that the privilege of some people and not others?"

❊ Ayatollah Sayyed Ali Khamenei, religious authority in Iran: "We are neither with you nor with the terrorists…. They [America] expect the entire world to help them because their interests demand it. Do they ever care about others' interests? These are the characteristics that make America so hated in the world."

None of these statements expresses threats that any group or faction is setting out to conquer the United States, force it to change its society, or impose its own ways of thinking on us. As far as I know, there have been no such statements. The September attacks were not aimed at targets like the Statue of Liberty but at structures that symbolize U.S. economic and military power.

How do Americans respond to this type of criticism? Righteous indignation is natural but not very productive over time. We need to examine such statements and try to understand the context out of which they come. It is not appeasement to search for knowledge we do not currently have. How can such acts be prevented from happening again if the real reasons for the acts are left undiscovered—or worse, ignored?

In my opinion one of the most tragic aspects of this trauma has been that thousands of families are bereaved, forever, and they do not know why this happened to them. Perhaps this book can help.

Understanding Arabs provides background and context for increasing cultural awareness, but it was written years before the problem of world terrorism assumed its present proportions. It was written primarily as a guide for Westerners, particularly Americans. To make the book more relevant to the current situation and to broaden the intended audience, I offer here some salient points that I believe must be considered as the world's people decide how as nations they will cope with this emergent threat. My purpose is to list what I believe to be objective facts rather than to interject recommendations or to suggest specific solutions.

* Mainstream Muslims do not approve of this terrorist group's acts. In fact they are horrified. The decision to engage in terrorism was the response of a singularly misguided cult-mentality group. Terrorism is in no way supported by the doctrines of the Islamic religion, which has always placed emphasis on human relationships and social justice. (There is much material on this topic, some of it available on the Internet.)

  Al Qaeda group members have disguised themselves as immigrants, thus taking advantage of the good reputation Mideastern immigrants have earned. As a group, the immigrants are known to be industrious and family-centered. The terrorists betrayed these people. They posed as immigrants who wanted to share in the bounties of the West, but from the very beginning the terrorists had an entirely different agenda.

* Mainstream Muslims do not want to change Western (or other non-Muslim) cultures. Many Muslims do not want Western values to enter their own societies, but providing their own lives are not affected, Muslims (and Mideasterners in general) are not concerned with how Westerners and others structure their own lives. The vast majority do not resent Western prosperity and freedom; in fact, millions of them immigrate to the West because they admire many of the social values and want to participate in a Western way of life. They want their children to grow up free and with the possibility of prosperity.

* We must not allow a cult to represent an entire religion. The bombing of abortion clinics is not justified by mainstream Christian faith. Sectarian violence in Ireland does not represent mainstream Protestantism or Catholicism.

* Muslims, Arabs, and other Mideasterners do not blame Americans as individuals. Their assumption, right or

wrong, is that the people of the United States cannot be held personally responsible because they are generally unaware of their government's policies. Americans are known to other nations as being uninformed. (Less obvious to Mideasterners is the fact that many Americans, at least prior to 11 September, also didn't care.) Unlike the terrorists' sympathizers, most Mideasterners have genuinely grieved for innocent lives lost in this or in any violent warlike act. They are like people everywhere.

✳ The 11 September attack was not a real Jihad. The term *Jihad*, as used in mainstream Islam, is misunderstood. Its primary meaning is not "Holy War," although that has become its meaning in Western languages. Most pertinent here, a true Jihad must be a response to an attack or threat made by non-Muslims toward the Muslim community. *Muslims may not initiate a Jihad.*

The terrorists are trying to promote enmity between Islam and Christianity. They are misusing the term *Jihad* just as they misuse terms like *Crusade, infidel,* and *unbeliever.* The term *Jihad* has become politicized and is constantly being invoked and misused for political purposes. During the war between Iraq and Iran, for example, each declared a Jihad against the other.

✳ The Qur'an and other Muslim sacred scriptures, like those of other religions, are long, complex, and open to wide-ranging interpretations. Emphasis on details such as presumed rewards in Paradise for people who die in a Jihad are, frankly, irrelevant and insulting to most educated Muslims. Muslims are not religiously motivated in any way to harm or kill non-Muslims. As with any body of sacred scripture, a selective choice of quotes can "prove" anything, including completely opposite ideas.

✳ Focusing on Al Qaeda and Islamic terrorists is too narrow a goal. It will not end the threat. These terrorists are short-term enemies, current targets against whom the United States now wages war. But even if they are eliminated, *the root causes of resentment will continue to exist.* The U.S. must reverse the negative perceptions about itself, and this cannot be done by force. No security is effective enough to prevent an attack by a person who is willing to commit suicide. Long-term strategic thinking is needed.

Sweeping statements that are frightening but do not suggest a remedy are not a solution. What use are statements such as "All humanity is at risk" and "You will never take down this great nation" and "What the United States has done to attract violent attacks is to be strong, wealthy, and successful"? If Americans blindly declare that the terrorists hate them for their benevolence, successes, and innocence, where does it lead? It does not help in framing an appropriate response.

If the United States and the Western world continue to ignore accusations, especially those they do not fully understand, they do so at their own peril. What brings forth statements that America is "morally corrupt and hypocritical"? Why is America accused of "supporting state-sponsored terrorism"? Why is there cheering when someone says "Americans never see the blood"? These are the types of statements that must be thoughtfully considered if there is to be any hope of a just and lasting peace.

* * * * * * *

Thousands of innocent citizens have died. More may follow. What should be done?

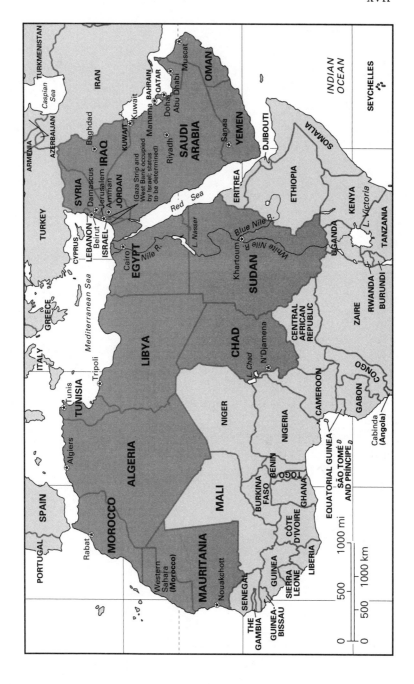

Preface

This book deals with Arab countries (defined as Arabic-speaking) in the Middle East. It does *not* discuss the non-Arab but primarily Muslim countries of the Middle East—Turkey (where the inhabitants speak a language of Mongolian origin), Iran, Pakistan, or Afghanistan (where people, including the Kurds, speak Aryan languages, which are part of the Indo-European language family).

We must not confuse Arabs with Muslims. Muslims are the majority in at least 55 countries; 18 to 20 of these are Arab countries (depending on one's definition). There are 1.3 billion Muslims in the world and about 220 million Arabs (5 percent of whom are Christian).*

Islam is the world's fastest-growing religion. Owing to immigration, Islam has become the second-largest religion in both the United States and Europe. Three-fourths of the refugees in the world are Muslims (UNHCR 2001).

The shared origins of Christianity and Islam have often been overshadowed by the historical conflicts between the two—"the Crusader mentality," "the clash of civilizations." The parallel concepts of Jihad (when equated with Holy

---

* A full, detailed map of the Islamic world and its peoples may be found in the January 2002 issue of *National Geographic*.

War) and Crusade not only resemble each other, *they are essentially equivalent* and distinguish these two faiths from other major world religions. Ancient rivalries and modern-day conflicts have accentuated the differences and polarized the West and the Mideast, obscuring the shared beliefs of the three great interrelated monotheistic faiths—Judaism, Christianity, and Islam.

The purpose of this book is to provide a cross-cultural guide for foreigners who are living in an Arab country, who encounter Arabs frequently, or who are interested in the behavior of Arabs, whether encountered in the media or personally. It is written particularly for Westerners—North Americans and Europeans—and underlines the contrasts between Western and Arab societies. It is for nonspecialists who want to have a clearer understanding of the thought patterns, social relationships, and ways of life of modern Arabs. The book also includes information about modern Islam.

Most of us are aware of the degree to which different national and cultural groups stereotype each other, even in person-to-person relations. When Westerners and Arabs interact, especially if neither understands the other, they often come away with impressions that are mutually negative.

It has been said that Americans, in particular, lack a historical consciousness of the rest of the world (Hanafi 1992). And when it comes to the Middle East, most Westerners know biblical history better than contemporary history. *This is misleading,* because the Arabs and Israelis of today are not the same people referred to in the Bible. Many Israelis are of European and other non-Semitic origins, and the Palestinians are Arabs but not Arabians from the Arabian Peninsula; they are descended from indigenous populations such as Canaanites, Moabites, Jebusites, Phoenicians, and other such groups. The current conflict has its origins entirely in the twentieth century.

It is my hope that this book will help alleviate that problem in two ways: (1) by explaining some of the behavioral characteristics of Arabs in terms of cultural background, thereby deepening the reader's understanding and helping to avoid negative interpretations and (2) by serving as a guide to cross-cultural interaction with Arabs, which will help people avoid inadvertent insults and errors of etiquette.

Foreigners find very little material available to help them understand Arab society. Not much has been written on the subject of Arab cultural and social practices, either in Arabic or in Western languages. A great deal of the material that exists is over thirty years old and appears dated to anyone who is familiar with Arab society today. Some observations made only twenty years ago are no longer applicable. In recent years changes in education, housing, health, technology, and other areas have also caused marked changes in attitudes and customs.

The most serious deficiency in research about Arab society is the lack of attention given to modern, urban (and often Western-educated) Arabs. Researchers, especially anthropologists, have mostly focused on village life and nomadic groups and on the study of traditional social patterns. Interesting as these studies are, they offer little directly applicable information for Westerners who will, for the most part, observe or interact with Arabs who are well educated, well traveled, and sophisticated.

This book is an attempt to fill that gap. It focuses on the socially elite—businessmen and -women, bureaucrats, managers, scientists, professors, military officers, lawyers, banking officials, and intellectuals—and the ways in which they interact with foreigners and with each other. In most Arab countries the elite differ considerably from rural or tradition-oriented social groups; indeed, some types of behavior required by the norms of one group are considered obsolete by another. At the same time, many basic traditions and customs still determine the way of life of all Arabs and affect their goals, values, and codes of accepted behavior. The many similarities among social groups and among the various Arab countries still outweigh the differences, so valid generalizations are possible. Any significant differences among groups will be pointed out.

It is important that Westerners who interact with upper-class, educated Arabs be aware of the particular characteristics of Arab etiquette and patterns of behavior and thought, since the differences may be quite subtle and, initially, hard to identify. It is easy to be lulled into the security of assuming that the superficial similarities of appearance, dress, and lifestyle among educated Arabs mean that they are "just like us." One is more likely to remain alert for differing social proprieties when seated in a tent or a mud-floor village house; it is not so easy to remember the differences when seated in the living room of a modern home, surrounded by Western-style furnishings and English-speaking Arabs.

I realize that any attempt to describe the motives and values of an entire people is risky. On the one hand, it leads to generalizations that are not true in all cases, and, on the other, it necessarily involves the observer's perspectives and interpretations and leads to emphasizing some traits over others. I have tried to present a balanced view, one that is generally descriptive of Arabs throughout the entire cultural area of the "Arab World." Most of the material in this book comes from my own personal experiences and from interviews with others. These interviews have taken place in virtually all of the Arab countries—in North Africa, the Levant, the Fertile Crescent, and the Arabian Peninsula.

It would be tempting simply to list all the charming, attractive, and admirable qualities found in Arab society and let it go at that, but this is not a book written for tourist agencies. That kind of information, while interesting, is generally of little practical value to a person who must live in Arab society and/or interact with Arabs on a regular basis about substantive matters. To be of real value in helping people deal with cross-cultural relationships in the Arab World, we must look at as many differences as possible and focus especially on problem areas, not on the delightful surprises awaiting the foreigner (the wonderful food, the kindness to children and elderly people, the lack of violent crime). It is the problem areas that need our attention, study, and thought; to leave them out would be to shortchange the reader *and perhaps lead to serious errors in judgment when interacting with Arabs.* Philip A. Salem, an Arab American, has written a thoughtful article about what Arabs and Americans can learn from each other (1995). The author suggests that these Arab values can be offered to the West: spiritual and human values, family values, long-term friendships, generosity of heart, and a deeper meaning of life. Arabs could learn from these Western values: respect for science, commitment to hard work and discipline, commitment to promises, the art of listening, tolerance for opposing views, teamwork, and objectivity.

The Arabs have been subjected to so much direct or indirect criticism by the West that they are very sensitive to a Westerner's statements about them. I have made an effort to be fair and honest and, at the same time, sympathetic to the Arab way of life, especially when contrasting Arab and Western cultural behavior. I have described differences while trying to avoid value judgments; there is no assumption that one cultural approach is superior to the other.

Note: the Arabic words that appear in this book are not written in detailed phonemic transcription. They are spelled with conventional English letters and are an approximation of the way the words should be pronounced. Arabic words may be spelled in varying ways in English. In each of the pairs used as examples here, the second spelling is closer to the actual Arabic pronunciation: Moslem/Muslim, Mohammed/Muhammad, Koran/Qur'an. *Al* is the Arabic word for "the," also spelled "El." It can be written with or without a hyphen connecting it to the next word.

I owe thanks to many people whose insights and stories contributed to this book. To all the students, diplomats, military officers, and businesspeople with whom I spent hours discussing cultural and social experiences, thank you.

In particular, I wish to acknowledge my late husband, Carl, for his assistance in all phases of preparation of the first edition of this book. Parts of the manuscript were read by Les Benedict, Helen Edwards, John McCaffrey, Mary Joy McGregor, Janet Schoenike, and Grace Shahid, all of whom offered valuable comments and suggestions. I also thank Dr. George Selim of the Library of Congress and Dr. Mahmoud Esmail Sieny of King Saud University for their assistance. The second and third editions were prepared with the much-appreciated editorial assistance of Carleton S. Coon, Jr. A large part of the research on Islam and Muslims in the West was done by Al-Husein Madhany.

Most of all, I thank the Arabs. My experiences with them over the years have added much pleasure and richness to my life.

—Margaret K. (Omar) Nydell

Introduction: *Patterns of Change*

Arab society has been subjected to enormous pressures from the outside world, particularly since the Second World War. Social change is evident everywhere because the effects of economic modernization have been felt in all areas of life. Even for nomads and residents of remote villages, the traditional way of life is disappearing.

Modernization

Most social change has come through the adoption of Western technology, consumer products, health-care systems, financial structures, educational concepts, and political ideas. These changes, necessarily, are controversial but inevitable and are present to varying degrees in all of the Arab countries.

The Arab nations have experienced an influx of foreign advisers, managers, businesspeople, teachers, engineers, health-care and military personnel, politicians, and tourists. Through personal contacts and increased media exposure, Arabs have been learning how outsiders live. Thousands of Arab students have been educated in the West and have returned with changed habits and attitudes. The spread of the Internet will have a major impact as well.

1

Arab governments are building schools, hospitals, housing units, and industrial complexes so fast that entire cities and towns change their appearance in a few years. It is easy to feel lost in some Arab cities if you have been away only a year or two. Modern hotels are found in any large Arab city; the streets and roads are full of cars; and the telephone, fax, and airline services are often overtaxed. Imported consumer products are abundant in most Arab countries, ranging from white wedding dresses to goods in supermarkets. While these are surface changes, they symbolize deeper shifts in values.

Overall rates of literacy have increased dramatically. In the last forty years, the number of educated people doubled in some Arab countries and increased ten times or more in others. Literacy rose from less than 10 percent in the Arabian Peninsula in the 1940s to 65–85 percent in 1998* and has increased by the same ratio among rural people in most of the Arab countries. Among urban people, it has reached 80 percent or more almost everywhere (Maddy-Weitzman 1998).

The rise in literacy is due to a phenomenal growth in public education, which is free and mandatory in all Arab countries. In Saudi Arabia enrollment in primary schools has more than doubled since 1980 (*Regional Surveys: The Middle East and North Africa* 1995). In 1980, 5 to 7 years of schooling was average; this increased to 9 to 10 years by 1997 (*World Development Report* 2000/2001). Enrollment went from 50,000 in 1983 to 113,000 in 1989 (Metz 1993), and by 1998 it was 165,000 (*The Middle East and North Africa 2001* 2001, 1034). In Kuwait there were 3,600 students in schools in 1945 (primary and secondary), 270,000 in 1994, and 288,500 in 1997 (*Regional Surveys*, 624). Saudi Arabia had 3,107 schools in 1970 and 20,000 in 1997 (*The Middle East and North Africa 2001*, 1029).

Education at the university level is growing even faster than at primary and secondary levels, sometimes doubling or

---

* Except in Yemen, where the literacy rate is approximately 38 percent.

tripling in one or two decades. These are percentages of eligible students enrolled at the university level in their home countries (*The Middle East and North Africa 2001* 2001; *Middle East Review* 2000):

Percentage Enrolled in University Education

	1980	2000
Egypt	16	23
Jordan	13	22
Kuwait	11	27
Morocco	6	11
Oman	0	8
Saudi Arabia	7	16
Tunisia	5	14

Arab women are becoming more educated and active professionally. Figures regarding women in the workplace have risen so rapidly that local censuses have not been able to keep pace with them. In 1973 only 7 percent of women were employed in the workforce (Fernea 2000, 30). Currently, the percentages of women in the workforce range from under 15 percent in some Gulf states to 30 percent and above in Morocco, Tunisia, and Egypt. In Kuwait women were nonexistent in the workforce until the early 1970s; now 31 percent of them work. These are statistics for 1998–1999 (*Middle East Review*):

Percentage of Women in the Workforce 1998–1999

Algeria	27
Egypt	30
Jordan	24
Lebanon	29
Morocco	35
Saudi Arabia	15

Syria	27
Tunisia	30
Yemen	28

Improved health care is changing the quality and length of life. The number of physicians per 1,000 people has skyrocketed in some Arab countries, doubling and almost tripling just since 1980 (*World Development Indicators* 2001).[†]

Number of Physicians per 1000 People

	1980	1998
Jordan	0.8	1.7
Oman	0.5	1.3
Syria	0.4	1.3
UAE	1.1	1.8

The number of hospital beds per 1000 people shows an equally dramatic increase. In Saudi Arabia this number rose from 11,400 in 1980 to 37,000 in 1990 to 46,000 in 1998 (Metz, 104; Saudi Arabian Information Resource 2001).

Life expectancy in the Arab countries has risen dramatically. Between 1955 and 1998, life expectancy rose from 43 to 67 years of age in Morocco, from 42 to 67 in Egypt, from 34 to 71 in Saudi Arabia, and from 55 to 77 in Kuwait (*World Factbook, 2001* 2001). This increased longevity is reflected in population statistics. Since the 1950s, the average rate of population growth has ranged between 2.5 and 3 percent, as high as anywhere in the world (Barakat 1993, 28). Between 1986 and 1990, alone, the overall Arab population grew by 5 to 7 percent (8 percent in the United Arab Emirates and 10 percent in Oman); it then leveled out to about 2 to 3 percent (Maddy-Weitzman, 189). In recent years, however, population growth has once again soared. In 1996 Oman and Gaza

---

[†] Comparative statistics are not available for many of the countries.

had the highest rates of natural growth (not counting migration) in the world, with 4.9 and 4.6 percent per year, respectively. Yemen, Syria, and Iraq grew at the rate of between 3.5 and 3.7 percent, also extremely high rates ("Population versus Peace" 1996). Estimates show that by 1998, 30 to 40 percent of the entire Arab population was under age fifteen; in Algeria it was 54 percent (*World Factbook, 2001*; Flanigan 2002; *Regional Surveys*, 332). The World Bank estimates that the population of the Middle East as a whole will increase two and a half times (from 448 million to 1.17 billion) between 2000 and 2100.

All over the Arab World, the population has been shifting from farms and villages to large urban centers, most dramatically during the period from the end of World War II through 1980. The magnitude of urbanization is illustrated by comparing urbanization rates between 1970 and 1998 (Department of International Economic Affairs 1989; *Middle East Review*; *World Development Report*).

Percentage Urbanized

	1970	1990	1998
Algeria	40	45	60
Egypt	42	49	45
Jordan	51	68	73
Lebanon	59	84	88
Libya	36	70	86
Morocco	35	48	58
Saudi Arabia	49	77	83
Syria	43	52	53
Tunisia	43	54	63

In the Gulf states, urbanization was greater than 80 percent.

Some of the other major social changes and trends in the Arab World include the following:

- Family planning is promoted and increasingly practiced in most Arab countries, and it is accepted as permissible by most Islamic jurists.
- People have far more exposure to newspapers, television, radio, computers, and the Internet.
- Entertainment outside the home and family is growing more popular.
- More people travel and study abroad.
- Parents are finding that they have less control over their children's choice of career and lifestyle.
- More people are working for large, impersonal organizations and industries.
- Business organizations are increasingly involved in international trade.
- Political awareness and participation have increased significantly.
- Arab governments are promoting the idea of national identity to replace regional or kin-group loyalty.
- Educational and professional opportunities for women have sharply increased.

The issue for Arabs is not whether they want modernization. The momentum cannot be stopped now. *The issue is whether they can adopt Western technology without also adopting the Western values and social practices that go with it*—whether they can modernize without losing cherished traditional values.

The Effects of Change

The disruptive effects of the sudden introduction of foreign practices and concepts on traditional societies are well known, and the Arabs have not been spared. The social strains among groups of people who represent different levels of education and Western exposure can be intense, the mutual frustrations existing to a degree that can hardly be imagined by Westerners.

Many younger Arabs admire and even prefer Western dress, entertainment, and liberal thought, to the distress of older or more traditional Arabs. The generation gap, which is widening in the Arab World, is excruciatingly painful for some communities and families. A Westernized Arab once equated the feelings of an Arab father whose son refuses to accept the family's choice of a bride with the feelings of a Western father who discovers that his son is on drugs.

A common theme of Arab writers and journalists is the necessity for scrutinizing Western innovations, adopting those aspects that are beneficial to their society (such as scientific and technical knowledge) and rejecting those that are harmful (such as a lessening concern for family cohesion or entertainment involving the consumption of alcohol).

Arabs have long been concerned with the Westernization that is often a part of modernization. They want to modernize, *but not at the expense of certain traditions. It is a mistake to assume that Arabs aspire to create societies and governments on Western models.* A representative passage is found in Dr. Ghazi A. Algosaibi's essay "Arabs and Western Civilization."

> To sum up: we must not take an attitude to the West based on sentiment, emotion or fanaticism. We must scrutinize the elements of Western civilization carefully, and in doing so learn from its sciences and identify in its intellectual heritage those areas which we may need to adopt or acquire. At the same time, we must recognize its callous traits so that we may repudiate them out of hand. Perhaps in such a balanced view there will be something that will help us to build anew in our land a new and vital Arab way of life comparable to that ancient civilization of ours which once led the whole world. (1982, 16–17)

The following excerpt from a long article by the Saudi ambassador to the United States, published in the *Washington Post*, adds emphasis to this concern.

"Foreign imports" are nice as shiny or high-tech "things." But intangible social and political institutions imported from elsewhere can be deadly. Ask the shah of Iran. A constant problem with so much of the West is the pervasive need for short-fused solutions and instant gratification. Our pace is more for long-distance running, for durability.

We Saudis want to modernize, but not necessarily Westernize. We respect your society even if we disagree on some matters, and we do. (Bin Sultan 1994)

This sense of foreign intrusion is summarized by Bernard Lewis:

Western political domination, economic penetration and—longest, deepest, and most insidious of all—cultural influence changed the face of the region and transformed the lives of its people, turning them in new directions, arousing new hopes and fears, creating new dangers and new expectations without precedent in their cultural past. (2002, 44)

Westerners promote democracy, but of their own kind: democracy based on the separation of church and state, a civil society governed by secular laws. Dr. Lewis again:

To a Western observer, schooled in the theory and practice of Western freedom, it is precisely the lack of freedom—freedom of the mind from constraint and indoctrination, to question and inquire and speak; freedom of the economy from corrupt and pervasive mismanagement; freedom of women from male oppression; freedom of citizens from tyranny—that underlies so many of the troubles in the Muslim world. (45)

Speaking as a Westerner, I find it hard to envision a modern society (a self-sustaining, competitive industrial and technological society) unless it is open, with industry privatized, individual initiative rewarded, and free markets and a global economy established. A government cannot forbid its citizens to hear and consider such options. Many of these issues cannot be answered by a religion, any religion.

Both modernist and traditionalist ways of thinking are present at the same time in modern Arab society, forming a dualism. Modern science and technology are taught side by side with traditional law and religious subjects.

The Muslim View

It is important to realize that interpretations of Islamic practices differ widely. Many of the practices that distinguish Mideastern countries stem from *local cultural practices* (family relationships, women's role in society, people's manner of dress, child-rearing practices, female circumcision), *not religion.* A Western scholar of Islam, Peter Clarke of King's College, University of London, has noted that practices based on culture do change among Muslims, especially those living outside their home countries. "This will eventually have a broad impact on Islam. When you get into customs, you run into all sorts of problems with modernity. I'm not afraid of strict Islam. I'm afraid of cultural Islam" (Fisher 2001).

Educated people want modernism, and most want social and political change, but the overwhelming majority of Muslim Arabs also want to keep their Islamic lifestyle. As stated by Professor John Voll, "The intellectuals in the Muslim world are striving for reforms that are both authentically Islamic and authentically modern" (Waldman 1995). An Egyptian lawyer stated, "We don't need a reformation. We need a renewal. We must renew the spirit of Islam by applying it to conditions of the day" (Waldman).

But determining how to achieve this will be difficult indeed. The resurgence of religion further supports the views of the traditionalists, who oppose any reinterpretations of Islam, and this group contains many government authorities, military officers, teachers, journalists, and intellectuals. In a way, rather than adjusting to the modern world, they insist on making the world adjust to their image of what it should be (Brown 2000, 91). They want truth, but they also demand "authenticity"; somehow, Islam must accommodate modernity, but modernity must also accommodate Islam (Moussalli 1999, 10, 181).

Halim Barakat describes modern Arab society as still burdened with fragmentation, authoritarianism, traditionalism, religious fundamentalism, patriarchy, erosion of a sense of shared civil society, pyramidal social-class structure, and dependency (6).

Dr L. Carl Brown speaks to the possibility of a new global order:

> If the West provides the fabric of material progress through development of technology, then Islam provides its humanizing factor, morality, which leads to spreading the positive aspect of material progress to all nations.... [The goal is] a universally moral and materially advanced global world order. This stands in contrast with current Western domination of technology and control over world capitals without a strong morality that takes into consideration the redistribution of wealth and the equality of nations. (186)

Benazir Bhutto characterized two groups of Muslims—reactionary and progressive:

> I would describe Islam in two main categories: reactionary Islam and progressive Islam. We can have a reactionary interpretation of Islam which upholds the status quo, or we can have a progressive interpretation of Islam which tries to move with a changing world, which believes in human dignity, which believes in consensus, and which believes in giving women their due right. (1998, 107)

There has long been discussion about how Islamic education could or should differ from Western education. Many books are published on this subject, and it is continuously discussed in the media. Of particular concern is how science and technology relate to traditional Islamic values and ways of looking at the world. At the first World Conference in Muslim Education, held in Mecca in 1977, this concern was addressed:

Education has been the most effective method of changing the attitudes of the young and thus leading them to accept and initiate social change. Modern Western education places an exaggerated emphasis upon reason and rationality and underestimates the value of the spirit. It encourages scientific enquiry at the expense of faith; it promotes individualism; it breeds skepticism; it refuses to accept that which is not demonstrable; it is anthropocentric rather than theocentric. Even where it does not directly challenge faith, it relegates it to the background as something much less important than reason.

The content of education...can be divided for a Muslim into two categories: experience in the form of skills or technical knowledge whose nature varies from age to age and which is bound to change constantly; and experience based on certain constant or permanent values embodied in religion and scripture.... Believing as it does that the true aim of education is to produce men who have faith as well as knowledge, the one sustaining the other, Islam does not think that the pursuit of knowledge by itself without reference to the spiritual goal that man must try to attain, can do humanity much good. Knowledge divorced from faith is not only partial knowledge, it can even be described as a kind of new ignorance....

The spirit of Islam should, therefore, be the dominant feature in all textbooks on whatever subject. Moreover, all our courses, books, and teaching materials should have as their central theme the relationship between God, Man and the Universe. (Hussain and Ashraf 1979, 37–38, 72).

Muslims believe that textbooks should be prepared so that they reflect the Islamic outlook even as they present pertinent modern theories and discoveries. One educator suggested, for example, that, in the natural sciences, the word *nature* be replaced with *Allah* so that it is clear that God is the source of natural growth and development, of the properties of chemicals, of the laws of physics and astronomy, and the like. Historical events are to be evaluated not for military or political significance but by their success in furthering the spiritual aims of humanity; for example, an agnostic society that amassed a great empire would not be judged as "successful" (Qutb 1979, 56–60).

The relationship between Islam and science is uncertain—some assert that "Islamic science" does not exist, because Islam does not encourage free, creative inquiry; others are confident that the two can be reconciled (Hoodbhoy 1991, ix; Bakar 1999). Science involves prediction and control and is not concerned with an organic, spiritual universe, nor does it address the concept of a Creator (Hoodbhoy, 13). It is well known that Arab Muslim culture led to brilliant scientific inquiry in medieval times, upon which the European Renaissance was built. But it is less successful today, and some assert that religion "dampens the skeptical spirit necessary for science" (Overbye 2001). Others blame the emphasis on rote learning and authoritarianism in both religious and secular education. Science and religion have different purposes, Dr. Muzaffar Iqbal of the Center for Islam and Science in Canada explained. "Modern science doesn't claim to address the purpose of life; that is outside its domain. In the Islamic world, purpose is integral, part of that life" (Overbye).

There have been several Islamic summits with the aim of achieving greater political unity among Muslim nations. Especially recently, Arab governments have found themselves severely criticized and even openly challenged if they are viewed as too liberal or too cooperative with the West.

It is not surprising that the sentiments of some groups are increasingly anti-Western and that statements and actions are directed against Western governments, cultural symbols, and even individuals. Many indigenous social ills are blamed, with varying degrees of plausibility, on the West.

In his book *Science, Technology, and Development in the Muslim World*, Ziauddin Sardar quotes from the prospectus of the Muslim Institute. This passage illustrates one trend in the thinking of conservative Muslims.

Muslims have for about 200 years suffered a period of continuous and rapid decline in all fields of human endeavor—economic, social, political, and intellectual—and have been surpassed by a rival and mostly hostile civilization of the West.

The Western civilization (including the communist experiment) has predictably failed to provide mankind with a viable framework for social harmony, moral and spiritual fulfillment and satisfaction, and international peace; Western civilization has in fact created more problems of greater complexity for mankind than those it may have solved.... The social relationship of Islam, on the other hand, would allow for even greater material well-being in a harmonious social order which is also free of conflicts between men, groups of men, factors of production, or nations.... The Muslims' quest for "modernization" and "progress" through the Westernization of Muslim individuals and Muslim societies was, therefore, bound to fail and has done so at great cost to Muslim culture and the economic, social, and political fabric of Muslim societies.... The damage to Muslim societies is so extensive that it may not be possible, or even desirable, to repair or restore their existing social orders; the only viable alternative is to conceive and create social, economic, and political systems which are fundamentally different from those now prevailing in Muslim societies throughout the world. (1977, 55–56)

Muslim intellectuals are actively seeking an Islamic alternative for their societies. In many countries young people belong to informal Islamic groups in which there is much discussion about the role and contribution of Islam to society. As one writer summarized,

> It is merely a historical accident that makes Islam appear to be struggling between two dominant ideologies [capitalism and Marxism]. For within the Islamic process itself there is a dynamic revitalizing force not only to keep Islam alive but which provides it with generative creativity to re-establish itself as a well-defined system with solutions that are original to current problems. (El Guindi 1981, 23)

Outside pressure toward change is glaringly visible in the changes in Arab architecture and city planning. Skyscrapers and air conditioning have replaced thick-walled traditional houses that were designed to condition the air themselves. Many crowded "old city" districts, with twisted lanes and jumbled markets and houses, have been destroyed; those that are left are in stark contrast with the newer parts of cities, built with wide streets on a rectangular city-block plan. Some modern houses and apartments do not address the needs of families or communities—there is no daily gathering place for women or separate living and entertainment areas for men and women. It is difficult nowadays for an extended family to find housing in one place or even in one area.

Most Arabs who are well educated and engaged in professional work have learned to balance the demands of modern life with traditional values and concerns. Arab women may be doctors or scientists, but they still acknowledge their place in the family structure and believe in the need to guard their reputations carefully.

Many young people in particular agonize about their identity (family? nation? Arab region? religious group or secular?) and what constitutes appropriate lifestyle choices, a dilemma that is simply unknown among Westerners. Balancing between the "modern" (often Westernized) and the "authentic" (traditional) is a concern among Arabs in all levels of society.

Westerners see a dual personality present in many educated Arabs who have the ability to synthesize two diverse ways of thinking and appreciate both.

Fundamentalism (Islamism)

An increasing number of Muslim Arabs have reacted, especially since the 1970s, to the invasion of Western values and customs through what we in the West often call "Islamic fundamentalism." (More accurate terms are "Islamism," "militant Islam," or even "deviant Islam.") The vast majority of Muslims find no basis in the fundamental teachings and principles of Islam for extremist belief; therefore, "Islamic extremism," "Islamic fundamentalism," and the like do injustice to mainstream Islam and to the majority of Muslims in the world.[‡]

The mood for Islamic revival takes many forms, only some of which can properly be considered Islamist, but there is a common thread these days, throughout the Arab countries and indeed in other Muslim states: the rejection of Western morals and codes of behavior where they conflict with Islamic traditions. Islam is not just a religion in the Western sense; it prescribes proper behavior patterns for much of the everyday life of its followers, and in many cases these prescriptions differ from Western practices.

Even young and relatively well-educated Muslims often find themselves torn between two quite different value systems. Some seek a synthesis. Others, who may be alienated from their own governments and may feel rejected by the West, choose the route of total commitment to traditional Islamic values and hostility toward Western culture. They have no viable future in the current system (unemployment among young men can reach as high as 50 percent). The

---

[‡] Especially recommended is Karen Armstrong's *Islam* (2000)— the first chapter and the section on fundamentalism.

Islamic organizations that promote militant Islam may provide a haven where people can reinforce their identity, gain comfort and direction, and possibly acquire a measure of influence.[§] They help members with the psychological dislocation and cultural threat of their new environment; many of their members are so poorly educated that they are not aware of the deeper concepts of the religion they claim to defend. Islam is used as an avenue of protest against official corruption and socioeconomic injustice (Esposito 1999, 14). The overwhelming majority of these group members believe that *the West is inherently anti-Arab and anti-Muslim, that there is a de facto adversarial relationship.*

Clearly, the disproportionate focus on Islamic fundamentalism in the Western media has led to unwarranted images about the religion of Islam itself. At the Al-Janadriyya National Heritage and Culture Festival held in Riyadh in 1995, this was discussed by Dr. John Esposito, director of the Center for Muslim-Christian Understanding at Georgetown University:

> The focus on "Islamic fundamentalism" as a global threat has reinforced a tendency to equate violence with Islam, to fail to distinguish between the illegitimate use of religion by individuals and the faith and practice of the majority of the world's Muslims who, like believers in other religious traditions, wish to live in peace. To uncritically equate Islam and Islamic fundamentalism with extremism is to judge Islam only by those who wreak havoc, a standard not applied to Judaism and Christianity.

At the same conference, an interesting contrast was pointed out by Murad Hoffman, who noted that while, in the

---

[§] It is hard to define "fundamentalist" organizations, because they range across a wide spectrum. Some are listed in R. Hrair Dekmejian's *Islam in Revolution, Fundamentalism in the Arab World* (1995).

Western media, terrorist attacks in Northern Ireland or Spain are not committed by "fanatic" Protestants or Catholics or Basques or Catalonians, whenever Muslims use force, even in legitimate self-defense, the Western media are likely to qualify them as fanatics.

In every Arab country there has been a marked increase in activities and the use of symbolic gestures that reconfirm the traditional Arab and Islamic values. Many women are once again wearing floor-length, long-sleeved dresses and are covering their hair with a *Hejab*. (Note: Wearing a headscarf does not indicate sympathy with extremism. It is a personal or cultural decision as a symbol of a woman's modesty.) Religious studies have increased in universities, as has the publication of religious tracts, and more religious orations are heard in public. The number of religious broadcasts and Islamic newspapers and books tripled in the 1980s alone (Willis 1984). There has been a steady increase in Islamic-oriented organizations, laws, social welfare services, educational institutes, youth centers, banks, and publishers. Many Islamists have entered politics. Islamic activism has become broad-based and institutionalized (Esposito 1998a, 250).

In Arab politics there has been a resurrection of the term *Jihad* (usually mistranslated into English as Holy War, although it basically refers to the effort that a Muslim makes to live and structure his or her society on Islamic principles, a much more benign meaning). In January 2002, in the wake of the September tragedy, at a conference of the Muslim World League in Saudi Arabia, Muslim scholars defined *terrorism* and *Jihad*. *Terrorism* is defined as "unlawful action, acts of aggression against individuals, groups or states [or] against human beings including attacks on their religion, life, intellect, property or honor" (Bashir 2002). Terrorism is any violence or threat designed to terrorize people or endanger their lives or security. *Jihad* is "self-defense, meant for upholding right, ending injustice, ensuring peace and security and establishing mercy." The conferees urged Muslims in non-Islamic countries to "abide by the rules of residence and citizenship and uphold public order in these countries" (Bashir). In an interview, the Sheikh (religious authority) of Al-Azhar University in Cairo, the oldest and most prominent Islamic center of learning, was quoted as saying,

> Quite simply explained, "jihad" means finding the true path, rejecting bad habits and bad traditions. This [more widely known] kind of jihad, familiar to people as martial dispute, can be accepted only under very special circumstances. The most important meaning of the concept of jihad is to reform oneself and one's own spirit by becoming clear about all matters of faith, by convincing oneself, and by providing others with a good example. (Diehl 1984, 115)

Newly emerging interpretations of Muslim law are exemplified here in a statement by Tariq Ramadan, an authority on new Islamic thought:

> Muslims who are residents or citizens of a non-Islamic state should understand that they are under a moral and social contract with the country in which they reside. In other words, they should respect the laws of the country. (2002, 161)

Mainstream Muslim interpretations of religious law are in direct contrast with fundamentalist tenets, yet it is the latter that are most often mentioned in the media. One analyst has summarized the appeal of the Islamist (fundamentalist) alternative. As an ideology, Islamic fundamentalism

1. bestows a new identity upon a multitude of alienated individuals who have lost their social-spiritual bearings,
2. defines the worldview of the believers in unambiguous terms by identifying the sources of good and evil,

3. offers alternative modalities to cope with the harsh environment,

4. provides a protest ideology against the established order,

5. grants a sense of dignity and belonging and a spiritual refuge from uncertainty, and

6. promises a better life in a future Islamic utopia, possibly on earth and assuredly in heaven. (Dekmejian 1995, 49)

Central to many modern Islam-oriented reform movements is the firm belief that faith will reestablish God's sovereignty and law, bringing success, power, and wealth to the Islamic community. The weakness and subservience of Muslim societies must be due to the faithlessness of Muslims who have strayed from God's divinely revealed path. Restoration of Muslim pride, power, and rule (the past glory of Islamic civilization) requires a return to Islam (Esposito 1999, 132).||

In the early centuries, Islamic law allowed for new interpretations and regulations as needed.¶ In the nineteenth and twentieth centuries, various reform and revival movements attempted to offer Islamic responses to the challenges of a changing, Western-dominated world. Many militant groups, including Al Qaeda, are calling for a rigorous application of the Qur'an and Islamic law (Esposito 1998b). However, these laymen (nonclerics) have taken it upon themselves to apply Islamic laws without consulting scholars of Islam. They do

---

|| Fourteen core beliefs of fundamentalists are listed in Esposito (1998a), 240–41.

¶ There is a process of utilizing Islamic specialists to apply the invariant principles and regulations of Islamic texts to fit a particular circumstance, without actually changing the foundations of the faith. This intellectual analysis is known to Muslims as *Ijtihad*, and recognized scholars continue it to the present day.

not recognize any interpretations made by Islamic jurists over the centuries.** On 4 November 2001, speaking to journalists in Damascus, Amr Mousa, head of the Arab League, rejected Osama Bin Laden's call to war. He forcefully stated, "Bin Laden does not speak in the name of the Arabs and Muslims" (Ford 2001).

The effects of militant Islam are now being felt all over the world. Extreme Islamist groups are especially strong in Algeria, Sudan, Egypt, Tunisia, Jordan, Lebanon, and Saudi Arabia (Boullata 1990, 154). Certainly this is viewed with dismay and some fear on the part of many Western observers, although it need not be seen as entirely political or anti-Western.

Jorgen Nielsen, Director of the Center for the Study of Islam and Christian-Muslim Relations in England, has stated,

> The Islamist movements represent a desire for autonomy, dignity and self-respect [and] not a threat to the West. It is in Europe's long-term interest to welcome this.... The well-being and self-respect of the Muslim world is in our own interest. (Al-Janadriyya National Heritage and Culture Festival 1995)

Tolerant (liberal, progressive) Muslims, the overwhelming majority, lack the money, organization, access to publication in the media, and zeal to promote their views. Some are simply afraid. They are too often overlooked because they rarely carry out actions that are newsworthy. They recognize that it has become urgent that these views be publicized.

** A technical example is the much-quoted verse, "Kill the unbelievers wherever you find them." The context of this revelation was the fifteen-year persecution of the nascent Muslim community by enemies intent on eradicating it, and it was directed toward them; this verse in no way refers to noncombatant non-Muslims today. Riad Saloojee, Director of the Council on American-Islamic Relations, Canada, 2002.

Facing the Future

It is clear that a great deal of confusion and upheaval is still to be experienced. The ambivalence toward or rejection of liberal social change, particularly if it contradicts traditional Arab values, can be better understood by considering the questions it raises in the mind of the modern Arab: How do you compare the relative value of a communications satellite with the wisdom of a village elder? What good is a son who is a computer expert but lacks filial respect? How do you cope with a highly educated daughter who announces that she never intends to marry?

This is the context in which Westerners encounter Arabs today. Remembering it as you explore Arab culture and as you develop relationships with Arab acquaintances will help make your experience more comprehensible and the relationships you develop more rewarding.

1

\

Beliefs and Values

When we set ourselves the task of coming to a better understanding of groups of people and their culture, it is useful to begin by identifying their most basic beliefs and values. It is these beliefs and values that determine their outlook on life and govern their social behavior. We have to make broad generalizations in order to compare groups of people—here, Arabs and Westerners. Bear in mind that this generalizing can never apply to all individuals in a group; the differences among Arabs of some twenty nations are many, although all have an Arab identity.

Westerners tend to believe, for instance, that the individual is the focal point of social existence, that laws apply equally to everyone, that people have a right to certain kinds of privacy, and that the environment can be controlled by humans through technological means. These beliefs have a strong influence on what Westerners think about the world around them and how they behave toward each other.

Arabs characteristically believe that many, if not most, things in life are controlled, ultimately, by fate rather than by humans; that everyone loves children; that wisdom increases with age; and that the inherent personalities of men and women are vastly different. These beliefs play a powerful role in determining the nature of Arab culture.

One might wonder whether there is, in fact, such a thing as Arab culture, given the diversity and spread of the Arab region. Looking at a map, one realizes how much is encompassed by the phrase "the Arab World." The Arab countries cover considerable territory, much of which is desert or wilderness. Sudan is larger than all of Western Europe, yet its population is far less than that of France; Saudi Arabia is larger than Texas and Alaska combined, yet has slightly more than twenty million people. Egypt, with seventy million people, is 95 percent desert. One writer has stated, "A true map of the Arab World would show it as an archipelago: a scattering of fertile islands through a void of sand and sea. The Arabic word for desert is *sahara* and it both divides and joins" (Stewart 1972, 9–10). The political diversity among the Arab countries is also notable; governmental systems include monarchies, military governments, and socialist republics.

But despite these differences, the Arabs are more homogeneous than Westerners in their outlook on life. All Arabs share basic beliefs and values that cross national and class boundaries. Social attitudes have remained relatively constant because Arab society is conservative and demands conformity from its members. Arabs' beliefs are influenced by Islam, even if they are not Muslims (many family and social practices are cultural, some are pre-Islamic); child-rearing practices are nearly identical; and the family structure is essentially the same. Arabs are not as mobile as people in the West, and they have a high regard for tradition. One observer summarized the commonalities shared by all Arab groups: the role of the family, the class structure, religious and political behavior, patterns of living, the presence of change, and the impact of economic development on people's lives (Barakat 1993, 21).

Initially, foreigners may feel that Arabs are difficult to understand, that their behavior patterns are not logical. In fact, their behavior is quite comprehensible, even predictable. For the most part it conforms to certain patterns that make Arabs consistent in their reactions to other people.

It is important for the foreigner to be aware of these cultural patterns, to distinguish them from individual traits. By becoming aware of patterns, one can achieve a better understanding of what to expect and thereby cope more easily. The following lists of Arab values, religious attitudes, and self-perceptions are central to the fundamental patterns of Arab culture and will be examined in detail in subsequent chapters.

Basic Arab Values

- A person's dignity, honor, and reputation are of paramount importance, and no effort should be spared to protect them. Honor (or shame) is often viewed as collective, pertaining to the entire family or group.
- It is important to behave at all times in a way that will create a good impression on others.
- Loyalty to one's family takes precedence over personal needs.
- Social class and family background are the major determining factors of personal status, followed by individual character and achievement.

Basic Arab Religious Attitudes

- Everyone believes in God, acknowledges His power, and has a religious affiliation.
- Humans cannot control all events; some things depend on God's will, that is, fate.
- Piety is one of the most admirable characteristics in a person.
- There should be no separation between church and state; religion should be taught in schools and promoted by governments (this is the Islamic view, not necessarily shared by Arab Christians).

- Established religious beliefs and practices are sacrosanct; liberal interpretations that threaten them must be rejected.

Basic Arab Self-Perceptions

- Arabs are generous, humanitarian, polite, and loyal. Several studies have demonstrated that Arabs see these traits as characteristic of themselves and as distinguishing them from other groups (Melikian 1977).*

- Arabs have a rich cultural heritage, as is illustrated by their contributions to religion, philosophy, literature, medicine, architecture, art, mathematics, and the natural sciences (some of which were made by non-Arabs living within the Islamic Empire). Most of these outstanding accomplishments are largely unknown and unappreciated in the West.†

- Although there are many differences among Arab countries, the Arabs are a clearly defined cultural group and perceive themselves to be members of the Arab Nation (*al-umma al-'arabiyya*).

- The Arab peoples have been victimized and exploited by the West. For them, the experience of the Palestinians represents the most painful and obvious example.

---

* Levon Melikian studied the modal personality of some Arab students, searching for traits to define "national character." I administered a word-association test to a group of Lebanese university students in 1972. The most common responses associated with the word *Arabs* were "generous," "brave," "honorable," and "loyal." About half of the forty-three respondents added "misunderstood."

† This subject is thoroughly discussed by Omran in *Population in the Arab World*, 13–41. See also Dennis Overbye (2001).

The Gulf War may be viewed (in part) as a Western action to force Iraq's compliance regarding an internationally recognized border, in contrast with nonenforcement in the case of Israel.[‡]

- Indiscriminate imitation of Western culture, by weakening traditional family ties and social and religious values, will have a corrupting influence on Arab society.

- Arabs are misunderstood and wrongly characterized by most Westerners. Many people in the West are basically anti-Arab and anti-Muslim. Many Westerners do not distinguish between Arabs and Muslims (see Appendix A).

[‡] In a poll taken in 2001, 90 percent of the Egyptian, Lebanese, Saudi, Kuwaiti, and UAE residents placed the Palestine problem among their top three concerns (Pappas 2001). Eighty-three to 94 percent criticized U.S. policy but stated they love American music, movies, clothes, democracy, and freedom (McGrory 2002). When Saudis were asked the reasons for their attitude toward the United States, 86 percent mentioned politics; only 6 percent mentioned values (Telhami 2002).

2

Friends and Strangers

The Concept of Friendship

Relationships are very personalized in the Arab culture. Friendships start and develop quickly. But the Arab concept of friendship, with its rights and duties, is quite different from that in the West.

Westerners, especially Americans, usually think of a friend as someone whose company they enjoy. A friend can be asked for a favor or for help if necessary, but it is considered poor form to cultivate a friendship primarily for what can be gained from that person or his or her position. Among Arabs, also, a friend is someone whose company one enjoys. *However, equally important to the relationship is the duty of a friend to give help and do favors to the best of his or her ability.*

Differences in expectations can lead to misunderstandings and, for both parties, a feeling of being let down. The Westerner feels "set up" to do favors, and the Arab concludes that no Westerner can be a "true friend." In order to avoid such feelings, we must bear in mind what is meant by both sides when one person calls another friend.

Reciprocal Favors

For an Arab good manners require that one never openly refuse a request from a friend. This does not mean that the favor must actually be done, but rather that the response must not be stated as a direct no. If a friend asks you for a favor, do it if you can—this keeps the friendship flourishing. If it is unreasonable, illegal, or too difficult, the correct form is to listen carefully and suggest that while you are doubtful about the outcome, you will at least try to help. Later, you express your regrets and offer instead to do something else in the future. In this way you have not openly refused a favor, and your face-to-face encounters have remained pleasant.

I once talked to an Egyptian university student who told me that he was very disappointed in his American professor. The professor had gratefully accepted many favors while he was getting settled in Egypt, including assistance in finding a maid and buying furniture. When the Egyptian asked him to use his influence in helping him obtain a graduate fellowship in the United States, the professor told him that there was no point in trying because his grades were not high enough to be competitive. The Egyptian took this as a personal affront and felt bitter that the professor did not care about him enough to help him work toward a better future. The more appropriate cross-cultural response by the professor would have been to make helpful gestures; for example, helping the student obtain information about fellowships, assisting him with applications, and offering encouragement—even if he was not optimistic about the outcome.

A similar incident happened to an American military officer in Morocco, who became angry when his Moroccan neighbor asked him to buy some items from the local military exchange, which is illegal. When he bluntly refused, his neighbor was offended and the friendship was severely damaged.

In Western culture actions are far more important and

more valued than words. *In the Arab culture, an oral promise has its own value as a response.* If an action does not follow, the other person cannot be held entirely responsible for a "failure."

If you fail to carry out a request, you will notice that no matter how hopeful your Arab friend was that you would succeed, he or she will probably accept your regrets graciously without asking precisely why the favor could not be done (which could embarrass you and possibly force you to admit a failure). You should be willing to show the same forbearance and understanding in inquiring about one of your requests. Noncommital answers probably mean there is no hope. This is one of the most frustrating cultural patterns Westerners confront in the Arab World. You must learn to work with this idea rather than fighting against it.

When Arabs say yes to your request, they are not necessarily certain that the action will or can be carried out. Etiquette demands that your request have a positive response. The result is a separate matter. A positive response to a request is a declaration of intention and an expression of goodwill—no more than that. *Yes* should not always be taken literally. You will hear phrases such as *Inshallah* (If God wills) used in connection with promised actions. This is called for culturally, and it sometimes results in lending a further degree of uncertainty to the situation.

In his controversial book *The Arab Mind*, Dr. Raphael Patai discusses this characteristic in some detail.

> The adult Arab makes statements which express threats, demands, or intentions, which he does not intend to carry out but which, once uttered, relax emotional tension, give psychological relief and at the same time reduce the pressure to engage in any act aimed at realizing the verbalized goal.... Once the intention of doing something is verbalized, this *verbal* formulation itself leaves in the mind of the speaker the impression that he *has done* something about the issue at hand, which in turn psychologically reduces the importance

of following it up by actually translating the stated intention into action.... There is no confusion between words and action, but rather a psychologically conditioned substitution of words for action.... The verbal statement of a threat or an intention (especially when it is uttered repeatedly and exaggeratedly) achieves such importance that the question of whether or not it is subsequently carried out becomes of minor significance. (1973, 60, 64, 65)

Sometimes an Arab asks another person for something and then adds the phrase, "Do this for my sake." This phrasing sounds odd to a foreigner, especially if the persons involved do not know each other well, because it appears to imply a very close friendship. In fact the expression means that the person requesting the action is acknowledging that he will consider himself indebted to return the favor in the future. "For my sake" is very effective in Arab culture when added to a request.

An Arab expects loyalty from anyone who is considered a friend. The friend is therefore not justified in becoming indignant when asked for favors, since it should be understood from the beginning that giving and receiving favors is an inherent part of the relationship. Arabs will not form or perpetuate a friendship unless they also like and respect you; their friendship is not as calculated or self-serving as it may appear. The practice of cultivating a person only in order to use him or her is no more acceptable among Arabs than it is among Westerners.

Introductions

Arabs quickly determine another person's social status and connections when they meet. They will, in addition, normally give more information about themselves than Westerners will. They may indulge in a little (or a lot of) self-praise and praise of their relatives and family, and they may present a detailed account of their social connections. When

Westerners meet someone for the first time, they tend to confine personal information to generalities about their education, profession, and interests.

To Arabs information about family and social connections is important, possibly even more important than the information about themselves. Family information is also what they want from you. They may find your response so inadequate that they wonder if you are hiding something, while your impression is that much of what they say is too detailed and largely irrelevant. Both parties give the information they think the other wants to know.

Your Arab friends' discourse about their influence network is not bragging, and it is *not* irrelevant. This information may turn out to be highly useful if you are ever in need of high-level personal contacts, and you should appreciate the offer of potential assistance from insiders in the community. Listen carefully to what they have to say.

Visiting Patterns

Arabs feel that good friends should see each other often, at least every few days, and they offer many invitations to each other. Westerners who have Arab friends sometimes feel overwhelmed by the frequent contact and wonder if they will ever have any privacy. There is no concept of privacy among Arabs. In translation, the Arabic word that comes closest to *privacy* means "loneliness"!

A British resident in Beirut once complained that he and his wife had almost no time to be alone—Arab friends and neighbors kept dropping in unexpectedly and often stayed late. He said, "I have one friend who telephoned and said, 'I haven't seen you anywhere. Where have you been for the last three days?'"

By far the most popular form of entertainment in the Arab World is conversation. Arabs enjoy long discussions over shared meals or many cups of coffee or tea. You will be expected to reciprocate invitations, although you do not have to keep pace precisely with the number you receive. If you plead for privacy or become too slack in socializing, people will wonder if they have offended you, if you don't like them, or if you are sick. You can say that you have been very busy, but resorting to this too often without sufficient explanation may be taken as an affront. "Perhaps," your friends may think, "you are just too busy for us."

I once experienced a classic example of the Arab (and especially Egyptian) love of companionship in Cairo. After about three hours at a party where I was surrounded by loud music and louder voices, I stepped onto the balcony for a moment of quiet and fresh air. One of the women noticed and followed immediately, asking, "Is anything wrong? Are you angry at someone?"

A young Arab American was quoted as saying,

> In the United States...you can have more personal space, I guess is about the best way to put it. You have privacy when you want privacy. And in Arab society they don't really understand the idea that you want to be alone. That means that you're mad, you're angry at something, or you're upset and you should have somebody with you." (Shipler 1986, 387)

If you are not willing to increase the frequency or intensity of your personal contacts, you may hurt your friends' feelings and damage the relationship. Ritual and essentially meaningless expressions used in Western greeting and leave-taking, such as "We've got to get together sometime," may well be taken literally, and you have approximately a one-week grace period in which to follow up with an invitation before your sincerity is questioned.

Some Westerners, as they learn about the intricate and time-consuming relationships that develop among friends, decide they would rather keep acquaintances at a distance. If you accept no favors, you will eventually be asked for none, and you will have much more time to yourself, but you will soon find that you have no Arab friends. Arab friends are generous with their time and efforts to help you, are willing to inconvenience themselves for you, and are concerned about your welfare. They will go to great lengths to be loyal and dependable. If you spend much time in an Arab country, it would be a great personal loss if you develop no Arab friendships.

Business Friendships

In business relationships personal contacts are much valued and quickly established. Arabs do not fit easily into impersonal roles, such as the "business colleague" role (with no private socializing offered or expected) or the "supervisor/employee" roles (where there may be cordial relations during work hours but where personal concerns are not discussed). For Arabs, all acquaintances are potential friends.

A good personal relationship is the most important single factor in doing business successfully with Arabs. A little light conversation before beginning a business discussion can be extremely effective in setting the right tone. Usually Arabs set aside a few minutes at the beginning of a meeting to inquire about each other's health and recent activities. If you are paying a business call on an Arab, it is best to let your host guide the conversation in this regard—if he is in a hurry, he may bring up the matter of business almost immediately; if not, you can tell by a lull in the conversational amenities when it is time to bring up the purpose of your visit. If an Arab is paying a call on you, don't be in such a rush to discuss business that you appear brusque.

The manager of the sales office of a British industrial equipment firm based in Kuwait told me about his initial inability to select effective salesmen. He learned that the best salesmen were not necessarily the most knowledgeable, eager, or efficient but were instead those who were relaxed, personable, and patient enough to establish friendly personal relations with their clients.

You will find it useful to become widely acquainted in business circles, and if you learn to mix business with pleasure, you will soon see how the latter helps the former proceed. *In the end personal contacts lead to more efficiency than following rules and regulations.* This is proven over and over again, when a quick telephone call to the right person cuts through lengthy procedures and seemingly insurmountable obstacles.

Office Relations

When Westerners work with the same people every day in an office, they sometimes become too casual about greetings. Arabs are conscientious about greeting everyone they see with "Good morning" or "Good afternoon" if it is the first encounter of the day, and they will go out of their way to say "Welcome back" when you return after an absence. Some Westerners omit greetings altogether, especially if they are distracted or hurried, and Arab co-workers invariably take notice. They usually understand and are not personally offended, but they interpret it as a lack of good manners.

An American nurse at a hospital in Taif, Saudi Arabia, had an enlightening experience on one occasion when she telephoned her Saudi supervisor to report arrangements for an emergency drill. She was enumerating the steps being taken when the Saudi said, "That's fine, but just a moment— first of all, how are you today?"

If you bring food or snacks into the office, it is a good idea to bring enough to share with everyone. Arabs place great value on hospitality and would be surprised if you ate or drank alone, without at least making an offer to share with everyone. The offer is a ritual, and if it is obviously your lunch or just enough food for yourself, it is usually politely refused; it depends on the situation.

Remember to inquire about business colleagues and co-workers if they have been sick, and ask about their personal concerns from time to time. Arabs do mention what is happening in their lives, usually good things like impending trips, weddings, and graduations. You do not need to devote much time to this; it is the gesture that counts.

In Arab offices supervisors and managers are expected to give praise to their employees from time to time, to reassure them that their work is noticed and appreciated. Direct praise, such as "You are an excellent employee and a real asset to this office," may be a little embarrassing to a Westerner, but Arabs give it frequently. You may hear "I think you are a wonderful person, and I am so glad you are my friend" or "You are so intelligent and knowledgeable; I really admire you." Statements like these are meant sincerely and are very common.

I was once visiting an American engineering office in Riyadh and fell into conversation with a Jordanian translator. I asked him how he liked his work. He answered in Arabic so that the Americans would not understand, "I've been working here for four years. I like it fine, but I wish they would tell me when my work is good, not just when they find something wrong." Some Westerners assume that employees know they are appreciated simply because they are kept on the job, whereas Arab employees (and friends, for that matter) expect and want praise when they feel they have earned it. Even when the Westerner does offer praise, it may be insufficient in quantity or quality for the Arab counterpart.

Criticism

Arab employees usually feel that criticism of their work, if it is phrased too bluntly, is a personal insult. The foreign supervisor is well advised to take care when giving criticism. It should be indirect and include praise of any good points first, accompanied by assurances of high regard for the individual.

To preserve the person's dignity, avoid criticism in front of others, unless an intermediary is used (see below for further discussion of intermediaries). The concept of constructive criticism truly cannot be translated into Arabic—forthright criticism is almost always taken as personal and destructive.

The need for care in criticism is well illustrated by an incident that occurred in an office in Amman. An American supervisor was discussing a draft report at some length with his Jordanian employee. He asked him to rewrite more than half of it, adding, "You must have entirely misunderstood what I wanted." The Jordanian was deeply hurt and said to one of the other employees, "I wonder why he doesn't like me." A far better approach would have been, "You are doing excellent work here, and this is a good report. We need to revise a few things, however; let's look at this again and work through it together, so we can make it even better."

I remember overhearing a dramatic confrontation in an office in Tunis, when an American supervisor reprimanded a Tunisian employee because he continually arrived late. This was done in front of other employees, some of whom were his subordinates. The Tunisian flared up in anger and responded, "I am from a good family! I know myself and my position in society!" Clearly he felt that his honor had been threatened and was not at all concerned with addressing the issue at hand.

In her perceptive book *Temperament and Character of the Arabs*, Dr. Sania Hamady writes (perhaps overstating):

Pride is one of the main elements on which Arab individual-ism rests, since it is sheer being which is primarily respected. To establish a good rapport with an Arab one must be aware of the fact that foremost in the Arab's view of the self is his self-esteem. It is important to pay tribute to it and to avoid offending it. The Arab is very touchy and his self-esteem is easily bruised. It is hard for him to be objective about himself or to accept calmly someone else's criticism of him.... Facts should not be presented to him nakedly; they should be masked so as to avoid any molestation of his inner self, which should be protected. (1960, 99)

Intermediaries

The designation of one person to act as an intermediary between two other persons is very common in Arab society. Personal influence is helpful in getting decisions made and things done, so people often ask someone with influence to represent them (in Arabic an intermediary is called a *wasta*).

If you are a manager, you may find that some employees prefer to deal with you through another person, especially if that person knows you well. An intermediary may serve as a representative of someone with a request or as a negotiator between two parties in a dispute.

Mediation or representation through a third party also saves face in the event that a request is not granted, and it gives the petitioner confidence that maximum influence has been brought to bear. You may want to initiate this yourself if an unpleasant confrontation with someone appears necessary. But because you, as an outsider, could easily make a mistake in selecting an intermediary, it is best to consult with other Arab employees (of a higher rank than the person with whom you have a conflict).

Foreign companies have local employees on their staff who maintain liaisons with government offices and help obtain permits and clearances. The better acquainted the employee is with government officials, the faster the work will be done and the better the service will be. Arab "government relations" employees are indispensable; no foreigner could hope to be as effective with highly placed officials.

You will observe the wide use of intermediaries in Arab political disputes. Mediators, such as those who undertake shuttle diplomacy, are often essential in establishing the personal contact that makes consensus possible. Their success depends on the quality of the personal relationship they establish with the parties involved. If mediators are recognized by both parties as being honorable and trustworthy, they have already come a long way in solving the problem. That is why some negotiators and diplomats are far more effective than others; personalities and perceptions, not issues, determine their relative success.

An outstanding example of diplomatic success due, in large part, to personality may be seen in Henry Kissinger's achievements when he served as a negotiator between the leaders of Syria, Egypt, and Israel after the 1973 War. He established personal friendships with the individuals involved; Anwar Sadat's remark that "Dr. Henry is my friend" is very revealing. These friendships contributed greatly to Kissinger's ability to discuss complicated issues and keep a dialogue going, something no one had managed to do before.

On the political level, you will constantly see situations in which an individual Arab leader attempts to mediate disputes among other Arab governments.

Private and Public Manners

In the Arab way of thinking, people are clearly divided into friends and strangers. The manners required when dealing with these two groups are very different. With friends and personal acquaintances, it is essential to be polite, honest, generous, and helpful at all times. When dealing with strangers, "public manners" are applied and do not call for the same kind of considerateness.

It is accepted practice to do such things as crowd into lines, push, drive aggressively, and overcharge tourists. If you are a stranger to the person or persons you are dealing with, then they will respond to you as they do to any stranger. Resenting this public behavior will not help you function better in Arab societies, and judging individuals as ill-mannered because of it will inhibit the development of needed relationships.

All over the Arab World people drive fast, cross lanes without looking, turn corners from the wrong lane, and honk their horns impatiently. Yet, if you catch a driver's eye or ask his or her permission, the driver will graciously motion for you to pull ahead or will give you the right-of-way.

While shopping in a tourist shop in Damascus, I watched a busload of tourists buy items at extremely high prices. When they were gone, I chatted with the shopkeeper for a few minutes and then bought some things. After I had left, a small boy came running after me—the shop owner had sent him to return a few more pennies in change.

Whenever I am in a crowded airport line, I try to make light conversation with the people around me. Never has anyone with whom I talked tried to push in front of me; in fact, they often motion for me to precede them.

Personal contact makes all the difference. If you feel jostled while you are waiting in line, the gentle announcement "I was here first" or "Please wait in line" will usually produce an apology, and the person will at least stand behind you. Keep calm, avoid scenes, and remember that none of the behavior is directed at you personally.

3

Emotion and Logic

How people deal with emotion or what value they place on objective versus subjective behavior is culturally conditioned. *While objectivity is given considerable emphasis in Western culture, the opposite is true in Arab culture.*

Objectivity and Subjectivity

Westerners are taught that objectivity, the examination of facts in a logical way without the intrusion of emotional bias, is the mature and constructive approach to human affairs. One of the results of this belief is that in Western culture, subjectivity—a willingness to allow personal feelings and emotions to influence one's view of events—represents immaturity. Arabs believe differently. They place a high value on the display of emotion, sometimes to the embarrassment or discomfort of foreigners. It is not uncommon to hear Westerners label this behavior as immature, imposing their own values on what they have observed.

A British office manager in Saudi Arabia once described to me his problems with a Palestinian employee. "He is too sensitive, too emotional about everything," he said. "The first thing he should do is grow up." While Westerners label Arabs as too emotional, Arabs may find Westerners cold and inscrutable.

Arabs consciously reserve the right to look at the world in a subjective way, particularly if a more objective assessment of a situation would bring to mind a too-painful truth. There is nothing to gain, for example, by pointing out Israel's brilliant achievements in land reclamation or in comparing the quality of Arab-made consumer items with imported ones. Such comments will generally not lead to a substantive discussion of how Arabs could benefit by imitating others; more likely, Arab listeners will become angry and defensive, insisting that the situation is not as you describe it and bringing up issues such as Israeli occupation of Arab lands or the moral deterioration of technological societies.

Fatalism

Fatalism, or a belief that people are powerless to control events, is part of traditional Arab culture. It has been much overemphasized by Westerners, however, and is far more prevalent among traditional, uneducated Arabs than it is among the educated elite today. Nevertheless, it still needs to be considered, since it is often encountered in one form or another.

For Arabs, fatalism is based on the belief that God has direct and ultimate control of all that happens. If something goes wrong, people can absolve themselves of blame or can justify doing nothing to make improvements or changes by assigning the cause to God's will. Indeed, too much self-confidence about controlling events is considered a sign of arrogance tinged with blasphemy. The legacy of fatalism in Arab thought is most apparent in the ritual phrase "Inshallah," noted in chapter 2.

Western thought has essentially rejected fatalism. Although God is believed by many Westerners to intervene in human affairs, Greek logic, the humanism of the Enlightenment, and cause-and-effect empiricism have inclined the West to view humans as having the ability to control their environment and destiny.

What Is Reality?

Reality is what you perceive—if you believe something exists, it is real to you. If you select or rearrange facts and if you
repeat these to yourself often enough, they eventually become reality.

The difference between Westerners and Arabs arises not
from the fact that this selection takes place, but from the
manner in which each makes the selection. Arabs are more
likely to allow subjective perceptions to determine what is
real and to direct their actions. This is a common source of
frustration for Westerners, who often fail to understand why
people in the Middle East act as they do. This is not to say
that Arabs cannot be objective—they can. But there is often
a difference in outward behavior.

If Arabs feel that something threatens their personal dignity, they may be obliged to deny it, even in the face of facts
to the contrary. A Westerner can point out flaws in their
arguments, but that is not the point. If they do not want to
accept the facts, they will reject them and proceed according
to their own view of the situation. Arabs will rarely admit to
errors openly if doing so will cause them to lose face. *To
Arabs, honor is more important than facts.*

An American woman in Tunis realized, when she was
packing to leave, that some of her clothes and a suitcase were
missing. She confronted the maid, who insisted that she had
no idea where they could be. When the American found
some of her clothes under a mattress, she called the company's
Tunisian security officer. They went to the maid's house and
found more missing items. The maid was adamant that she
could not account for the items being in her home. The
security officer said that he felt the matter should not be
reported to the police; the maid's humiliation in front of her
neighbors was sufficient punishment.

An American diplomat recounted an incident he had observed in Jerusalem. An Israeli entered a small Arab-owned

cafe and asked for some watermelon, pointing at it and using the Hebrew word. The Arab proprietor responded that it should be called by the Arabic name, but the Israeli insisted on the Hebrew name. The Arab took offense at this point. He paused, shrugged, and instead of serving his customer, said, "There isn't any!"

At a conference held to discuss Arab and American cultures, Dr. Laura Nader related this incident.

> The mistake people in one culture often make in dealing with another culture is to transfer their functions to the other culture's functions. A political scientist, for example, went to the Middle East to do some research one summer and to analyze Egyptian newspapers. When he came back, he said to me, "But they are all just full of emotions. There is no data in these newspapers." I said, "What makes you think there should be?" (in Atiyeh 1977, 179)

Another way of influencing the perception of reality is by the choice of descriptive words and names. The Arabs are very careful in naming or referring to places, people, and events; slogans and labels are popular and provide an insight into how things are viewed. The Arabs realize that *names have a powerful effect on perception.*

There is a big psychological gap between opposing labels like "Palestine/Israel," "The West Bank/Judea and Samaria," and "freedom fighters ("hero martyrs" if they are killed)/terrorists." The 1967 Arab-Israeli War is called in Arabic The War of the Setback—in other words, it was not a "defeat." The 1973 War is called The War of Ramadan or The Sixth of October War, not The Yom Kippur War.

Be conscious of names and labels—they matter a great deal to the Arabs. If you attend carefully to what you hear in conversations with Arabs and what is written in their newspapers, you will note how precisely they select descriptive words and phrases. You may find yourself being corrected by Arab acquaintances ("It is the Arabian Gulf, not the Persian

Gulf," for example), and you will soon learn which terms are acceptable and which are not.

The Human Dimension

Arabs look at life in a personalized way. They are concerned about people and feelings and place emphasis on human factors when they make decisions or analyze events. They feel that Westerners are too prone to look at events in an abstract or theoretical way and that most Westerners lack sensitivity toward people.

In the Arab World, a manager or official is always willing to reconsider a decision, regulation, or problem in view of someone's personal situation. Any regulation can be modified or avoided by someone who is sufficiently persuasive, particularly if the request is justified on the grounds of unusual personal need. This is unlike most Western societies, which emphasize the equal application of laws to all citizens. *In the Arab culture, people are more important than rules.*

T. E. Lawrence stated it succinctly: "Arabs believe in persons, not in institutions" (1926, 24). They have a long tradition of personal appeal to authorities for exceptions to rules. This is commonly seen when they attempt to obtain special permits, exemptions from fees, acceptance into a school when preconditions are not met, or employment when qualifications are inadequate. They do not accept predetermined standards if these standards are a personal inconvenience.

Arabs place great value on personal interviews and on giving people the opportunity to state their case. They are not comfortable filling out forms or dealing with an organization impersonally. They want to know the name of the top person who makes the final decision and are always confident that the rejection of a request may be reversed if top-level personal contact can be made. Frequently, that is exactly what happens.

Persuasion

Arabs and Westerners place a different value on certain types of statements, which may lead to decreased effectiveness on both sides when they negotiate with each other. Arabs respond much more readily to personalized arguments than to attempts to impose "logical" conclusions. When you are trying to make a persuasive case in your discussions with Arabs, you will find it helpful to supplement your arguments with personal comments. You can refer to your friendship with each other or emphasize the effect approval or disapproval of the action will have on other people.

In the Middle East, negotiation and persuasion have been developed into a fine art. Participants in negotiations enjoy long, spirited discussions and are usually not in any hurry to conclude them. Speakers feel free to add to their points of argument by demonstrating their verbal cleverness, using their personal charm, applying personal pressure, and engaging in personal appeals for consideration of their point of view.

The display of emotion also plays its part; indeed, one of the most commonly misunderstood aspects of Arab communication involves their "display" of anger. Arabs are not usually as angry as they appear to be. Raising the voice, repeating points, even pounding the table for emphasis may sound angry, but in the speaker's mind, they merely indicate sincerity. A Westerner overhearing such a conversation (especially if it is in Arabic) may wrongly conclude that an argument is taking place. *Emotion connotes deep and sincere concern for the substance of the discussion.*

Foreigners often miss the emotional dimension in their cross-cultural transactions with Arabs. A British businessman once found that he and his wife were denied reservations on a plane because the Arab ticketing official took offense at the manner in which he was addressed. The fact that seats were available was not an effective counterargument. But when the Arab official noticed that the businessman's wife had begun to cry, he gave way and provided them with seats.

Arabs usually include human elements in their arguments. In arguing the Palestine issue, for instance, they have often placed the greatest emphasis on the suffering of individuals rather than on points of law or a recital of historical events. This is beginning to change, however, with a growing awareness of how to relate effectively to the way Westerners think and argue.

4

ع

Getting Personal

The concept of what constitutes personal behavior or a personal question is culturally determined, and there are marked differences between Westerners and Arabs. This is a subject that is rarely discussed openly, since how one defines what is personal or private seems so natural to each group. On the whole, Westerners feel that Arabs become too personal, too soon.

Personal Questions

Arabs like to discuss money and may ask what you paid for things or what your salary is (this is more common among less Westernized people). If you don't wish to give out the information, consider responding without answering. You can speak on the subject of money in general—how hard it is to stay ahead, high prices, inflation. After a few minutes of this, the listener will realize that you do not intend to give a substantive answer. This is the way Arabs would respond if they were asked a question they did not really want to answer.

If you are unmarried or if you are married and childless, or have no sons, Arabs may openly ask why. They consider it unusual for an adult to be unmarried, since marriage is ar-

51

ranged for many people by their families and, in any event, is expected of everyone. People want children, especially sons, to enhance their prestige and assure them of care in their old age.

Unmarried people may well find themselves subjected to well-intentioned matchmaking efforts on the part of Arab friends. If you wish to avoid being "matched," you may have to resort to making up a fictitious long-distance romance! You might say, "I am engaged and we're working out the plans. I hope it won't be long now." Statements such as "I'm not married because I haven't found the right person yet" or "I don't want to get married" make little sense to many Arabs.

When you explain why you don't have children, or more children, don't say "We don't want any more children" (impossible to believe) or "We can't afford more" (also doubtful). A more acceptable answer is "We would like more children, and if God wills, we will have more."

Questions that Arabs consider too personal are those pertaining to women in the family (if asked by a man). It is best to ask about "the family," not a person's wife, sister, or grown daughter.

Sensitive Subjects

There are two subjects that Arabs favor in social conversation—religion and politics—and both can be risky.

Muslims enjoy discussing religion with non-Muslim Westerners because of their curiosity about Western religious beliefs and because they feel motivated to share information about Islam with friends as a favor to them. They are secure in their belief about the completeness of Islam, since it is accepted as the third and final refinement of the two previously revealed religions, Judaism and Christianity. They like to teach about Islam, which eventually leads to the question: why don't you consider conversion? A Westerner may feel uncomfortable and wonder how to give a gracious refusal. The simplest, most gracious, and most acceptable answer is to state that you appreciate the information and respect Islam highly as a religion but that you cannot consider conversion because it would offend your family. Another option is to assure people that you are a serious, committed Christian (if this is the case). There is a widespread perception that most Westerners are not religious; if you are, people will be very impressed.

Arabs like to talk politics with Westerners and readily bring up controversial issues like the Palestine problem and the legacy of colonialism and imperialism. Yet they are not prepared for frank statements of disagreement with their positions on these questions or even inadvertent comments that sound negative toward their point of view or supportive of the opposing side of the argument. The safest response, if you cannot agree fully, is to confine yourself to platitudes and wait for the subject to change, expressing your concern for the victims of war and your hope for a lasting peace. *A frank, two-sided discussion is usually not constructive if the subject is an emotional one*, and you may find that Arabs remember only the statements you made in support of the other side.

You will be able to tell when you have brought up a sensitive subject by the way your Arab friend evades a direct answer to your questions. If you receive evasive answers, don't press further; there is a reason why the person does not want to pursue the subject. John Laffin has described a discussion with the late Kamal Nasir, who was the press officer for the Palestine Liberation Organization.

> Nasir, a likeable but nervy man, put his hands to his head in despair. "Do you know, Arafat has never said either 'yes' or 'no' to me when I ask him a direct question. You would think he could do that much for his Press officer!" I sympathized with him. "Do you like Arafat?" I asked. And Nasir replied, "It's not a matter of liking or disliking."

> In my three long talks with him [Nasir], he, too, never once said "yes" or "no." (1975, 78–79)

It is useful to introduce other topics into the conversation if you can, to change the subject. These are suggested topics that most people love to discuss:

- the Golden Age of the Arabs and their contributions in the Middle Ages,
- the culturally required traits of an "ideal person,"
- the experience of making the Hajj (pilgrimage),
- the person's extended family, and
- the Arabic language, its literature, and poetry.

Social Distance

Arab and Western cultures differ in the amount of touching they feel comfortable with in interpersonal relations and in the physical distance they maintain when conversing. These norms are largely unconscious, so both Arabs and Westerners may feel uncomfortable without knowing exactly why.

In general Arabs tend to stand and sit closer and to touch other people (of the same sex) more than Westerners do. It is common to see two men or two women holding hands as they walk down a street, which is simply a sign of friendship. You must be prepared for the possibility that an Arab will take your hand, especially when crossing the street. After shaking hands in greeting, Arabs may continue to hold your hand while talking—if the conversation is expected to be brief. They will then shake it again when saying good-bye. Kissing on both cheeks is a common form of greeting (again, only with members of the same sex), as is embracing. It is also common to touch someone repeatedly during a conversation, often to emphasize a point. Children, especially if they are blond, should be prepared to have their heads rubbed by well-meaning adults.

Arab culture does not have the same concept of public and private space as do Western cultures. Westerners, in a sense, carry a little bubble of private space around with them. Arabs, on the other hand, are not uncomfortable when they are close to or touching strangers.

Westerners are accustomed to standing in an elevator in such a way that maximum space is maintained between people. In the Arab World it is common for a person to board an elevator and stand close beside you rather than moving to the opposite corner. When an Arab boards a bus or selects a seat on a bench, he often sits beside someone rather than going to an empty seat or leaving a space between himself and others. To give a typical example, this tendency was particularly annoying to an American who was standing on a street corner in Beirut waiting for a friend. He had a good view of the intersecting streets until a Lebanese man came to the corner and, apparently also waiting for someone, stood directly in front of him for no apparent reason. When Arabs and Westerners are talking, they may both continually shift position, in a kind of unconscious dance, as the Arab approaches and the Westerner backs away, each trying to maintain a comfortable distance. For Arabs the space that is comfortable for ordinary social conversation is approximately the same as that which Westerners reserve for intimate conversation.

Anthropologist Edward T. Hall has described the Arab concept of personal space as follows:

For the Arab, there is no such thing as an intrusion in public. Public means public. In the Western world, the person is synonymous with an individual inside a skin. And in northern Europe generally, the skin and even the clothes may be inviolate. You need permission to touch either if you are a stranger.... For the Arab, the location of the person in relation to the body is quite different. The person exists somewhere down inside the body.... Tucking the ego down inside the body shell not only would permit higher population densities but would explain why it is that Arab communications are stepped up as much as they are when compared to northern European communication patterns. Not only is the sheer noise level much higher, but the piercing look of the eyes, the touch of the hands, and the mutual bathing in the warm moist breath during conversation represent stepped-up sensory inputs to a level which many Europeans find unbearably intense. (1966, 15)

Robert A. Barakat, in a study of Arab gestures, also discusses Arab body language.

All Arabs...share a certain basic vocabulary of body language. They stand close together and frequently touch each other in a conversation, and they look each other in the eye constantly, instead of letting their gaze drift to the side as Americans do. (1973, 65–66)

You do not need to adopt Arab touching patterns, of course; just be aware that they are different from your own and accept them as natural and normal. Note: in Saudi Arabia and the Arabian Peninsula countries, touching other people is not nearly so common and can even be offensive.

Gestures

Arabs make liberal use of gestures when they talk, especially if they are enthusiastic about what they are saying. Hand and facial gestures are thus an important part of Arab communication. If you are able to recognize them, you will be able to get the full meaning of what is being said to you.

Listed here are some of the most common gestures used in Arab countries. There are variations among countries, but most are in wide use. Men use gestures more than women do, and less educated people use them more than the educated do. You should not try to use these gestures (foreigners often use gestures in the wrong place or situation), but you should learn to recognize them.

1. Moving the head slightly back and raising the eyebrows: no. Moving the head back and chin upward: no. Moving the chin back slightly and making a clicking sound with the tongue: no.

2. After shaking hands, placing the right hand to the heart or chest: greeting someone with respect or sincerity.

3. Holding the right hand out, palm downward, and moving it as if scooping something away from you: go away.

4. Holding the right hand out, palm upward, and opening and closing it: come here.

5. Holding the right hand out, palm upward, then closing the hand halfway and holding it: give it to me.

6. Holding the right hand out, palm downward, and moving it up and down slowly: quiet down.

7. Holding the right hand out, palm upward, and touching the thumb and tips of fingers together and moving the hand up and down: calm down; be patient; slowly.

8. Holding the right forefinger up and moving it from left to right quickly several times (the "windshield wiper"): no; never.

9. Holding the right hand out, palm downward, then quickly twisting the hand to show the palm upward: what? why?

10. Making a fist with the right hand, keeping the thumb extended upward: very good; I am winning. (This is a victory sign. You may have seen this gesture made by Yasser Arafat when talking to the press.)

Names

In many Western societies, one indication of the closeness of a personal relationship is the use of first names. In Arab society the first name is used immediately, even if it is preceded by "Miss," "Mrs.," or "Mr."

Arabs do not refer to people by their third, or "last," name. Arab names, for both men and women, consist of a first name (the person's own), the father's name and the paternal grandfather's name, followed by a family name (in countries where family names are used). In other words an Arab's name is simply a string of names listing ancestors on the father's side. A Western example might be John (given name) Robert (his father) William (his grandfather) Jones.

Because names reflect genealogy on the father's side, women have masculine names after their first name. Some people include *ibn* (son of) or *bint* (daughter of) between the ancestral names. This practice is common in the Arabian Peninsula; for example, Abdel-Aziz ibn Saud (son of Saud), the founder of the Kingdom of Saudi Arabia. In North Africa the word *ben* or *ould* is used to mean "son of"; *bou* (father of) is also a common element of a family name. Examples are political figures such as Abdelaziz Bouteflika, the president of Algeria; Maaouya Ould Sidi Ahmed Taya, the president of Mauritania; and Zayn Al-Abdin Ben Ali, the president of Tunisia.

Because a person's first name is the only one that is really his or hers, Arabs use it from the moment they are introduced. A Western man can expect to be called "Mr. Bill" or "Mr. John." If he is married, his wife would be called "Mrs. Mary," or possibly "Mrs. Bill." An unmarried woman would be "Miss Mary." First names are also used with titles such as "Doctor" and "Professor."

A person may retain several names for legal purposes but will often omit them in daily use. A man named Ahmad Abdallah Ali Muhammad, for example, would be commonly known as Ahmad Abdallah; if he has a family or tribal name, let's say Al-Harithi, he would be known as Ahmad Abdallah Al-Harithi or possibly Ahmad Al-Harithi. Similarly, a woman whose full name is Zeinab Abdallah Ali Muhammad Al-Harithi may be known as Zeinab Abdallah or Zeinab Al-

Harithi. People are not always consistent when reciting their names on different occasions.

When a genealogical name becomes too long (after four or five generations), some of the older names will be dropped. The only pattern that is really consistent is that the father's name will be retained along with the family name, if there is one. It is entirely possible that full brothers and sisters may be registered with different combinations of names.

In Arabian Peninsula countries telephone books list people under their family names. In some Arab countries, however, the telephone book lists people under their first names, because the first name is the only one that can be depended on to be consistently present. Some business organizations find it easier to keep payroll records by first name.

A family or tribal name identifies a large extended family or group whose members still consider themselves tied by bonds of kinship and honor. A family name may be geographical (Hijazi, "from Hijaz"; Halaby, "from Aleppo"); denote an occupation (Haddad, "smith"; Najjar, "carpenter"); be descriptive (Al-Ahmar, "red"; Al-Tawil, "tall"); denote tribe (Al-Harithi; Quraishi); or sound like a personal name because it is the name of a common ancestor (Abdel-Aziz; Ibrahim).

An Arab Muslim woman does not change her name after marriage, since she does not take her husband's genealogy. Arabs are very proud of their mother's family and want her to retain the name and refer to it. Only informally is a wife called "Mrs." with her husband's first or last name.

When people have children, an informal but very pleasing and polite way to address the parents is by the name of the oldest son or oldest child: *abu* (father of) or *umm* (mother of) the child; for example, Umm Ahmad (mother of Ahmad). These terms of address are considered respectful, and *umm* is especially useful when talking to a woman because it provides a less personal way of addressing her.

Arabs do not name their sons after the father, but naming a child after his paternal grandfather is common. You will meet many men whose first and third names are the same.

Titles are used more widely in Arabic than in English. Anyone with an M.D. or Ph.D. degree must be addressed as "Dr." (*duktoar* for a man, *duktoara* for a woman). It is important to find out any titles a person may have; omitting the title can be insulting. "Sheikh" is a respectful title for a wealthy, influential, or elderly man. Government ministers are called *Ma'ali*, and senior officials are given the honorary title *Sa'ada* before their other titles and name.

Most Arab names have a meaning and can be clues to certain facts about a person. Many names indicate religion or country of origin. Because the exchange of personal information is so important, some people introduce themselves with various long combinations of names, especially if their first and last names are ambiguous (used by more than one group).

It is useful for foreigners to be able to place people, at least partially, upon hearing their names. Here are a few guidelines.

1. If a name sounds Western (George, William, Mary), it marks a Christian.

2. If a name is that of a well-known figure in Islamic history (Muhammad, Bilal, Salah-Eddeen, Fatima, Ayesha), it marks a Muslim.

3. Most hyphenated names using "Abdel-" are Muslim. The name means "Servant (Slave) of God," and the second part is one of the attributes of God (Abdallah, "Servant of Allah"; Abdel-Rahman, "Servant of the Merciful"; Abdel-Karim, "Servant of the Generous"). There are a few Christian names on this pattern (Abdel-Malak, "Servant of the Angel"; Abdel-Massih, "Servant of the Messiah"), but over 90 percent of the time you can assume that a person with this type of name is Muslim. Of the ninety-nine Muslim attributes for God (the All-Powerful,

All-Knowing, All-Compassionate, All-Wise, etc.), most are currently in use as names.

4. Names containing the word *Deen* (religion) are Muslim (Sharaf-Eddeen, "The Honor of Religion"; Badr-Eddeen, "The Moon of Religion"; Sayf-Eddeen, "The Sword of Religion").

5. Many names are simply descriptive adjectives (Aziz, "powerful"; Said, "happy"; Amin, "faithful"; Hasan, "good"). Such descriptive names do not mark religion.

6. Names that derive from both the Qur'an and the Bible (Ibrahim, "Abraham"; Sulaiman, "Solomon"; Daoud, "David"; Yousef, "Joseph") do not distinguish whether the person is Muslim, Christian, or Jewish.

5

Men and Women

In Arab society the nature of interaction between men and women depends on the situation. Continual interaction is expected at work or in professional situations (although it remains reserved by Western standards, and in Saudi Arabia is actually restricted), but social interaction is very carefully controlled. The degree of control differs among Arab countries, depending on their relative conservatism, but nowhere is it as free and casual as in Western societies.

Social Interaction

The maintenance of family honor is one of the highest values in Arab society. Since misbehavior by women is believed to do more damage to family honor than misbehavior by men, clearly defined patterns of behavior have been developed to protect women (in the traditional view) and help them avoid situations that may give rise to false impressions or unfounded gossip. Women interact freely only with other women and close male relatives.

Arab men and women are careful about appearances when they meet. They avoid situations where they would be alone together, even for a short time. It is improper to be in a room together with the door closed, to go out on a date as a couple, or to travel together, even on a short daytime trip. Shared activities take place with other people present. At mixed social events women are accompanied by their husbands or male relatives. In Saudi Arabia "religious police" often question couples who are at a restaurant or in a car together and ask for proof that they are married.

Foreigners must be aware of the restrictions that pertain to contact between Arab men and women and then consider their own appearance in front of others. *Arabs quickly gain a negative impression if you behave with too much (presumed) familiarity toward a person of the opposite sex.* They will interpret your behavior on their own terms and may conclude that you are a person of low moral standards. If an embarrassing incident involves a Western man and an Arab woman, they may feel that the Westerner insulted the woman's honor, thereby threatening the honor of her family.

A Western man can feel free to greet an Arab woman at a social gathering (though it is not a common practice in Saudi Arabia), but their subsequent discussion should include other people rather than just the two of them. A married Western woman may greet and visit with Arab men, provided she is accompanied by her husband. If a woman is unmarried or if her husband is not present, she should be more reserved. In many Arab countries, men and women separate into their own conversation groups shortly after arrival at a social gathering; this depends on the customs of a given area. In Saudi Arabia women are often excluded from social gatherings altogether, or they may be more restricted in their behavior when they are included. It is important to point out that social separation is not practiced merely because it is required by custom; it is often preferred by both men and women because they feel more comfortable. Westerners can expect to spend much of their social time in all-male or all-female groups.

Western men and women should also give thought to their appearance in front of others when they interact among themselves. Behavior such as overly enthusiastic greetings, animated and joking conversations, and casual invitations to lunch are easily misinterpreted by Arabs and reinforce their stereotype of the morally lax Westerner.

Displaying Intimacy

The public display of intimacy between men and women is strictly forbidden by the Arab social code, including holding hands or linking arms or any gesture of affection such as kissing or prolonged touching. Such actions, even between husband and wife, are highly embarrassing to Arab observers. A married couple was once asked to leave a theater in Cairo because they were seen holding hands.

This type of behavior is a particularly serious offense in Saudi Arabia, and incidents of problems and misunderstandings are frequent. One such incident occurred when an American woman was observed getting into a car with an American man, sliding over to his side, and kissing him on the cheek. A captain of the Saudi National Guard, who happened to see this, demanded proof that they were married. They were, but not to each other. The woman was deported, and the man, who compounded his problem by being argumentative, was sent to jail. Even behavior such as holding hands (especially among young people in the less traditional countries) is still viewed by most people with disapproval.

The Status of Women

The degree to which women have been integrated into the workforce and circulate freely in public varies widely among the Arab countries. In Lebanon, Jordan, Iraq, Egypt, and Tunisia, educated women are very active at all levels of society. Women have been heads of state in four non-Arab Islamic countries: Pakistan, Bangladesh, Indonesia, and Turkey. In Saudi Arabia, Yemen, and the Arabian Gulf states, few women have jobs outside the home; those who do, work only in all-female environments such as schools and banks for women, with the exception of those in the medical professions.

All Arab governments now strongly support efforts to increase women's educational opportunities. In 1956, many years before the issue gained its current prominence, the Tunisian president, Habib Bourguiba, instituted laws improving the legal status of women, ultimately becoming known as "Liberator of Women." Iraq revised personal status laws regarding marriage, child custody, and inheritance in 1959. Egypt and Iraq outlawed polygamy in 1998, and the practice is restricted to certain conditions in most other countries. In Morocco a woman can stipulate in her marriage contract that polygamy is grounds for divorce (Anderson 1976, 63).* In the past ten to twenty years, personal status laws have been revised to increase the legal rights of women in most Arab countries, either by supplementing or by reinterpreting traditional Islamic law. In virtually every Arab country today, the laws regarding women are being discussed and are subject to change. The role of women in Arab society and in Islam is by no means static or fixed (Fernea 2000, 27).

In traditional Arab society men and women have well-defined spheres of activity and influence. Do not assume that because Arab women are not highly visible in public, their influence is similarly restricted in private life.

Arab women have a good deal of power in decision making. They usually have the decisive voice in matters relating to household expenditures, the upbringing and education of children, and sometimes the arrangement of marriages. Men are responsible for providing for the family's material welfare; even if a woman has her own money, she need not contribute to family expenses. Most women in fact *do* have their own

---

* The law was enacted in 1976.

money, and Islamic religious law states clearly that they retain sole control over their money and inheritance after marriage.

The older a woman becomes, the more status and power she accrues. Men owe great respect to their mothers all their lives, and most make every effort to obey their mother's wishes, including her whims. All older women in the family are treated with deference, but the mother of sons gains even more status.

Arab women generally wear clothing that is at least knee-length and partially sleeved. The practice of wearing more conservative, floor-length, fully sleeved clothing is increasing, not decreasing, even in modern cities like Cairo and Amman, and use of the Hejab hair cover has increased enormously in the last twenty years. In fact, women's clothing is taking on political and social implications, "an outward sign of a complex reality" (Bowen and Early 1993, 120). In many countries conservative dress is most common among young, educated women. This issue is widely discussed and debated within families and different groups of friends.

Many Muslim women veil their faces, wholly or partially, in conservative countries such as Saudi Arabia, Kuwait, the Arabian Gulf states, Yemen, and Libya and to some degree in Morocco and Algeria (the veil is forbidden in Tunisia) (Fernea, 29). Veiling has almost disappeared except in rural areas or in very conservative families in such countries as Syria, Lebanon, Jordan, and Iraq. The Qur'an itself says nothing specific about veiling, although it does urge women to be modest in their dress. Veiling has always been a matter of local custom, not a religious requirement.

Tradition-oriented Arab men and women do not view social customs and restrictions as repressive but as an appropriate acknowledgment of the status and nature of women. They see the restrictions as providing protection for women so that they need not be subjected to the stress, competition, temptations, and possible indignities found in outside society. Most

Arab women feel satisfied that the present social system provides them with security, protection, and respect.

Some women, however, view their situation otherwise and have begun pressing for greater social, legal, and personal freedom. There has long been a trend toward relaxing some of the restrictions that regulate women's activities. Ever-increasing numbers of women are entering universities and the workforce. However, some counterpressure is being applied by conservative religious leaders to impose or reimpose restrictions.

Middle Eastern gender roles have traditionally been governed by a patriarchal kinship system that had already existed in the regions to which Islam spread. Many of the variations in the status of women are due to local traditions and social customs (such as covering the entire face). Men are expected to provide for their families; women, to bear and raise children; children, to honor and respect their parents and grow up to fulfill their adult roles (which includes marriage) (Bowen and Early, 77). It is important for an outsider to keep these points of view in mind when analyzing or discussing the status of Arab women.

Western Women

Western women find that they do not quite fit into Arab society; they are not accorded the rights of men but they are not considered bound by all the restrictions of Arab women either.

Western women are expected to behave with propriety, but they are not required to be as conservative as Arab women in dress or in public behavior. They need not veil in Saudi Arabia, for example, but must wear conservative street dress in all Arab countries. They may go shopping, attend public activities, or travel alone.

Arabs accept professional Western women and admire them for their accomplishments. Well-educated women find that their opinions are taken seriously, and they are often invited to all-male professional gatherings. When a woman has a work-related reason to call on someone or to be present at any event, she is almost always welcomed, and men are comfortable with her presence.

6
٦

Social Formalities and Etiquette

Social formalities and rules of etiquette are extremely important in Arab society. *Good manners constitute the most salient factor in evaluating a person's character.*

Hospitality

Arabs are generous in the hospitality they offer to friends and strangers alike, and they admire and value the same in others. *Generosity to guests is essential for a good reputation.* It is a serious insult to characterize someone as stingy or inhospitable.

Arabs assume the role of host or hostess whenever the situation calls for it—in their office, home, or shop. A guest never stays long without being offered something to drink, and it is assumed that the guest will accept and drink at least a small quantity as an expression of friendship or esteem. When you are served a beverage, accept and hold the cup or glass with your right hand.

No matter how much coffee or tea you have had elsewhere, never decline this offer (some shops and business offices have employees whose sole duty is to serve beverages to guests). Dr. Fathi S. Yousef, an Arab sociologist, has pointed out that an American would likely ask guests, "Would you care for coffee or tea?" using an intonation pattern which suggests that they may or may not want any refreshment. A Middle Easterner would ask, "What would you like—coffee or tea?" simply giving the guests a choice (1974, 386). If someone comes to a home or place of business while food is being served, the people eating always offer to share the food. Usually an unexpected guest declines, but the gesture must be made.

The phrase *Ahlan wa Sahlan* or *Marhaba* (Welcome) is used when a guest arrives, and it is repeated several times during a visit. A guest is often given a seat of honor (this is particularly common as a gesture to a foreigner), and solicitous inquiries are made about the guest's comfort during the visit. A typical description of Arab hospitality appears in the introduction to a phrase book entitled *Spoken Arabic:*

> Hospitality is a byword among [Arabs], whatever their station in life. As a guest in their homes, you will be treated to the kindest and most lavish consideration. When they say, as they often do, "My home is your home," they mean it. (Salah 1982, 4)

Regardless of pressing circumstances, an Arab would never consider refusing entrance to a guest, even if he or she is unexpected and the visit inconvenient. The only excusable circumstance would be if a woman (or women) were at home alone when a man dropped by—and then it would be the visitor who would refuse to enter, even if his prospective host were expected back very soon.

Arabs are proud of their tradition of hospitality and have many anecdotes illustrating it. A favorite is the story of the Bedouin who killed his last camel (or sheep) to feed his guest. Arabs expect to be received with hospitality when they are guests, and *your personal image and status will be affected by people's perceptions of your hospitality.*

The most important components of hospitality are welcoming a guest (including using the word *Welcome*), offering the guest a seat (in many Arab homes, there is a special room set aside for receiving guests, called the "salon"), and offering something to drink. As a host, stay with your guests as much as possible, excusing yourself for brief absences from the room as necessary.

Condon and Yousef provide a close-up view of how Arabs receive guests:

> Although the "salon" is a very important room in the home, it is not the most frequently used. It is, paradoxically, both focal and peripheral. It is the center of the family's formal social interactions with visitors, while it is physically located on the periphery of the home.... In such a layout, the guest knocks at the door and is led into the salon through the home or asked to please wait until the other door leading immediately to the salon is opened for him. The behavior reflects two of the primary cultural values of the area. The first is the preoccupation with the concept of face, facades, and appearances. The guest is exposed only to the most shining, formal, and stylized part of the home and gets to meet only the members whom the family intends for him to meet. On the other hand, relationships in the Middle East reflect contextual varieties of guest-host interactions with territorial expectations of welcome and hospitality on the part of the guest and situational obligations of maintaining the traditional image of an open house on the part of the host. Thus, in receiving the guest in the most distinguished part of the home and in having him meet only the members of the family dressed for the occasion, the guest is honored and the family status is reflected. (1977, 160)

Even as a tourist, you will be met with hospitality in the Arab World. If you ask directions, people will try to give you an answer (even if they don't know where your destination is!), or they will assist you in asking others; they might just take you to your destination themselves.

A friend of mine once made up a fictitious address in Riyadh and asked several people where it was; he got an answer every time. The crowning moment came when he asked two policemen, who simultaneously pointed in opposite directions.

In Tunis, Cairo, Beirut, and Amman I have asked for directions and been escorted to my destination though in each instance it was a long walk and a considerable inconvenience for my guide. When thanking someone for such a favor, you will hear the response, "No thanks are needed for a duty." No task is too burdensome for a hospitable host.

Time and Appointments

Among Arabs time is not as fixed and rigidly segmented as it tends to be among Westerners. It flows from past to present to future, and Arabs flow with it. Social occasions and appointments need not have fixed beginnings or endings. Arabs are thus much more relaxed about the timing of events than they are about other aspects of their lives. Nevertheless, these attitudes are beginning to change as people respond to the demands of economic and technological development and modernization.

Some Arabs are careful to arrive on time (and are impatient with those who do not), and some are habitually late, especially for social events. Given these attitudes, a person who arrives late and has kept you waiting may not realize that you have been inconvenienced and expect an apology.

Frequently, an Arab shopkeeper or someone in a service trade fails to have something finished by a promised time. This also pertains to public services (such as getting a telephone connected), personal services, bus and train departures, customer services (where standing in long lines can be expected), and bureaucratic procedures. Be flexible; everyone expects delays. You will appear unreasonably impatient and demanding if you insist on having things finished at a precise time.

If you invite people for dinner or a social event, do not expect all of your guests to arrive on time. A dinner should be served rather late, and social plans should always be flexible enough to accommodate latecomers.

The Arabic word *Ma'alish* represents an entire way of looking at life and its frustrations. It means "Never mind" or "It doesn't matter" or "Excuse me—it's not that serious." You will hear this said frequently when someone has had a delay, a disappointment, or an unfortunate experience. Rather than give in to pointless anger, Arabs often react to impersonally caused adversity with resignation and, to some extent, an acceptance of their fate.

Discussing Business

Arabs mistrust people who do not appear to be sincere or who fail to demonstrate an interest in them personally or in their country. They also don't like to be hurried or to feel they are being pressured into a business agreement. If they like you, they will agree to try to work out an arrangement or a compromise; if they do not like you, they will probably stop listening. *They evaluate the source of a statement or proposal as much as the content.*

Initial reactions by your Arab counterparts to your suggestions, ideas, and proposals can be quite misleading if taken at face value. Arabs are not likely to criticize openly but are more likely to hint that changes are needed or to give more subtle indications that the proposal is unacceptable—by inaction, for instance. They may promise to be in touch but fail to do so, or they might offer a radical counterproposal that may constitute a position from which compromise is expected. Don't take flattery and praise too seriously. It will more likely be adherence to good manners than an indicator of potential success in the business transaction. Some decisions simply require consultation with superiors (if you are not dealing with the top person). A noncommittal reaction to a proposal does not mean it has been rejected, nor does it guarantee ultimate acceptance. Only time will tell the outcome, with success dependent, more often than not, on patience and the cultivation of good personal relations.

Despite the frustration you may feel as the result of delays, *if you press for a specific time by which you want a decision, you may actually harm your chances of success.* Your counterpart may perceive it as an insult, especially if the person is a high-ranking manager or executive.

The vice president of an American engineering company was meeting with a high-level Saudi official in the Ministry of Planning in Riyadh. The company's local representative had been trying for several weeks to obtain approval of one of the company's proposals. The vice president decided at the meeting to request that the ministry give them a definite answer during the week he was to be in town. The Saudi looked surprised and appeared irritated, then answered that he could not guarantee action within that time period. The proposal was never approved.

If a decision is coming slowly, it may mean that the proposal needs to be reassessed. Do not expect to conclude all of your business at once, especially if several decisions are required. Patience and repeated visits are called for. Arabs have plenty of time, and they see little need to accommodate foreigners who are in a hurry.

Sharing Meals

Arabs enjoy inviting guests to their home for meals; you will probably be a guest at meals many times. Sharing food together provides an Arab host and hostess with a perfect opportunity to display their generosity and demonstrate their personal regard for you.

It is not an Arab custom to send written invitations or to request confirmation of acceptance. Invitations are usually verbal and often spontaneous.

If it is your first invitation, check with others for the time meals are usually served and for the time you are expected to arrive. Westerners often arrive too early and assume the meal will be served earlier than is customary. In most Arab countries (but not all), a large midday meal is served between 2:00 and 3:00 P.M., and a supper (with guests) is served about 10:00 or 11:00 P.M. Guests should arrive about two hours before the meal, since most of the conversation takes place before the meal, not after it. If the dinner is formal and official, you may be expected to arrive at the specified time, and you can expect the meal to end within an hour or two.

Arabs serve a great quantity of food when they entertain—indeed, they are famous for their munificence and very proud of it. They do not try to calculate the amount of food actually needed; on the contrary, the intention is to present abundant food, which displays generosity and esteem for the guests. (The leftover food does not go to waste; it is consumed by the family or by servants for several days afterward.)

Most foreigners who have experienced Arab meals have their favorite hospitality stories. For example, I was told about a banquet once given by a wealthy merchant in Qatar who was known for his largesse. After several courses the guests were served an entire sheep—one per person!

You can expect to be offered second and third helpings of food, and you should make the gesture of accepting at least once. Encouraging guests to eat is part of an Arab host or hostess's duty and is required for good manners. This encouragement to eat more is called *'uzooma* in Arabic, and the more traditional the host, the more insistently it is done. Guests often begin with a ritual refusal and allow themselves to be won over by the host's insistence. You will hear, for example,

"No, thanks."
"Oh, but you must!"
"No, I really couldn't!"

"You don't like the food!"
"Oh, but I do!"
"Well then, have some more!"

Water may not be served until after a meal is finished; some people consider it unhealthy to eat and drink at the same time. In any case Arab food is rarely "hot," although it may be highly seasoned.

A guest is expected to express admiration and gratitude for the food. Because you are trying to be polite, you will probably overeat. Many people eat sparingly on the day they are invited out to dinner because they know how much food will be served that evening. In Morocco a table is often set with several tablecloths, and one is removed after every course. Before you begin to eat, count the tablecloths!

When you have eaten enough, you may refuse more by saying *Alhamdu lillah* (Thanks be to God). When the meal is over and you are about to leave the table, it is customary to say *Dayman* (Always) or *Sufra dayma* (May your table always be thus) to the host and hostess. The most common responses are *Ti'eesh* (May you live) and *Bil hana wa shifa* (To your happiness and health).

After a meal, tea or coffee will be served, often presweetened. Conversation continues for a while longer, perhaps an hour, and then guests prepare to leave. In some countries, bringing a tray of ice water around is a sign that dinner is over and the guests are free to leave. In the Arabian Peninsula countries, incense or cologne may be passed around just before the guests depart.

When guests announce their intention to leave, the host and hostess usually exclaim, "Stay a while—it's still early!" This offer is ritual; you may stay a few more minutes, but the expression need not be taken literally, and it does not mean that you will give offense by leaving. Generally, you can follow the example of other guests, except that many Arabs prefer to stay out very late, so you may still be the first to leave. In most Arab countries you do not have to stay after midnight.

When you are invited to a meal, it is appropriate, although not required, to bring a small gift; flowers and candy are the most common.

If you invite Arabs to your home, consider adopting some of their mealtime customs; it will improve their impression of you.

In the countries of the Arabian Peninsula, women rarely go out socially. When you invite a man and his wife to your home, the wife may not appear. It depends largely on whether the couple is accustomed to socializing with foreigners and on who else will be there. It is considerate, when a man is inviting a couple, to say, "My wife invites your wife" and to volunteer information about who else is invited. This helps the husband decide whether he wishes his wife to meet the other guests, and it assures him that other women will be present. Don't be surprised if some guests do not come, or if someone arrives with a friend or two.

Always serve plenty of food, with two or three main meat dishes; otherwise you may give the impression of being stingy. I once heard an Egyptian describe a dinner at an American's home where the guests were served one large steak apiece. "They counted the steaks, and they even counted the potatoes," he said. "We were served baked potatoes—one per person!"

If you serve buffet style rather than a sit-down dinner with courses, your eating schedule will be more flexible and the visual impression of the amount of food served will be enhanced.

Give thought to your menu, considering which foods are eaten locally and which are not. Serve foods in fairly simple, easily recognizable form, so guests won't wonder what they are eating in a foreigner's home. Arabs usually do not care for sweetened meats or for sweet salads with the main meal.

Muslims are forbidden to eat pork. Some foreigners serve pork (as one of the choices at a buffet) and label it; this is not advisable, since it can be disconcerting to Muslim guests, who may wonder if the pork has touched any of the rest of the food.

The consumption of alcohol is also forbidden for Muslims. Do not use it in your cooking unless you either label it or mention it. If you cook with wine or other alcohol, you will limit the dishes available to your Muslim guests—it does not matter that the alcohol may have evaporated during cooking. If you wish to serve wine or alcoholic beverages, have non-alcoholic drinks available too.

Be sure to offer your guests second and third helpings of food. Although you don't have to insist vigorously, you should make the gesture. Serve coffee and tea at the end of a meal.

Smoking

The overwhelming majority of Arab adults smoke, although women seldom smoke in public. Smoking is considered an integral part of adult behavior and constitutes, to some extent, the expression of an individual's "coming of age." Arab men, in particular, view smoking as a right, not a privilege. Do not be surprised if you see people disregarding "no smoking" signs in airplanes, waiting rooms, or elevators.

Arabs are rarely aware that smoking may be offensive to some Westerners. You can ask someone to refrain from smoking by explaining that it bothers you, but he may light up again after a few minutes. If you press the point too strongly, you will appear unreasonable.

Rules of Etiquette

Listed below are some of the basic rules of etiquette in Arab culture.

- It is important to sit properly. Slouching, draping the legs over the arm of a chair, or otherwise sitting carelessly when talking with someone communicates a lack of respect for that person. Legs are never crossed on top of a desk or table when talking with someone.

- When standing and talking with someone, it is considered disrespectful to lean against the wall or keep one's hands in one's pockets.

- Sitting in a manner that allows the sole of one's shoe to face another person is an insult.

- Failure to shake hands when meeting or bidding someone good-bye is considered rude. When a Western man is introduced to an Arab woman, it is the woman's choice whether to shake hands or not; she should be allowed to make the first move. (Pious Muslims may decline to shake hands with a woman; this is not an insult.)

- Casual dress at social events, many of which call for rather formal dress (a suit and tie for men, a dress, high heels, and jewelry for women), may be taken as a lack of respect for the hosts. There are, of course, some occasions for which casual dress is appropriate.

- One who lights a cigarette in a group must be prepared to offer cigarettes to everyone.

- Men stand when a woman enters a room; everyone stands when new guests arrive at a social gathering and when an elderly or high-ranking person enters or leaves.

- Men allow women to precede them through doorways, and men offer their seats to women if no others are available.

- It is customary to usher elderly people to the front of any line or to offer to stand in their place. Elderly people should be greeted first.

- When saying good-bye to guests, a gracious host accompanies them to the outer gate, or to their car, or at least as far as the elevator in a high-rise building.

- If a guest admires something small and portable, an Arab may insist that it be taken as a gift. Guests need to be careful about expressing admiration for small, expensive items.

- In many countries gifts are given and accepted with both hands and are not opened in the presence of the donor.

- In some social situations, especially in public places or when very traditional Arabs are present, it may be considered inappropriate for women to smoke or to drink alcoholic beverages.

- When eating with Arabs, especially when taking food from communal dishes, guests should not use the left hand (it is considered unclean).

- At a restaurant, Arabs will almost always insist on paying, especially if there are not many people in the party or if it is a business-related occasion. Giving in graciously after a ritual offer to pay and then returning the favor later is an appropriate response.

- Arabs have definite ideas about what constitutes proper masculine and feminine behavior and appearance. They do not approve of long hair on men or mannish dress on and comportment by women.

- Family disagreements and disputes in front of others or within hearing of others are avoided by Arabs.

- People should not be photographed without their permission.

- Staring at other people is not usually considered rude or an invasion of privacy by Arabs (especially when the object is a fascinating foreigner). Moving away is the best defense.

- When eating out with a large group of people where everyone is paying his or her own share, it is best to let one person pay and be reimbursed later. Arabs find the public calculation and division of a restaurant bill embarrassing.

- Most Arabs do not like to touch or be in the presence of household animals, especially dogs. Pets should be kept out of sight when Arab guests are present.

It is impossible, of course, to learn all the rules of a culture. The safest course of action is to imitate. In a social situation with Arabs, *never be the first one to do anything!* In some situations, such as in the presence of royalty, it is incorrect to cross your legs; in some situations, in the presence of royalty or a high-ranking older man, for instance, it is even incorrect to smoke.

7

∨

The Social Structure

Arab society is structured into social classes, and individuals inherit the social class of their family. The governments of Libya and the former South Yemen have tried experimenting with classless societies, but this has not affected basic attitudes.

Social Classes

In most Arab countries there are three social classes. The upper class includes royalty (in some countries), large and influential families, and some wealthy people, depending on their family background. The middle class is composed of government employees, military officers, teachers, and moderately prosperous merchants and landowners. Peasant farmers and the urban and village poor make up the lower class. Nomadic Bedouins do not really fit into any of these classes; they are mostly independent of society and are admired for their preservation of Arab traditions.

The relative degree of privilege among the classes and the differences in their attitude and way of life vary from country to country. Some countries are wealthy and underpopulated, with a large privileged class; others are poor and overpopulated, with a high percentage of peasants and manual laborers.

There is usually very little tension among social classes. Arabs accept the social class into which they were born, and there is relatively little effort on the part of individuals to rise from one class to another. In any case it would be difficult for a person to change social class, since it is determined almost entirely by family origin. One can improve one's status through professional position and power, educational attainment, or acquired wealth, but the person's origins will be remembered. A family of the lower class could not really expect social acceptance in the upper class for two or three generations. Similarly, an upper-class family that squandered its wealth or influence would not be relegated to lower-class status for some time.

Foreign residents of Arab countries automatically accrue most of the status and privileges of the upper class. This is due to their professional standing, their level of education, and their income.

Image and Upper-Class Behavior

Certain kinds of behavior are expected of people in the upper class who wish to maintain their status and good public image. Some activities are not acceptable in public and, if seen, cause shock and surprise.

If you know the basic norms of upper-class behavior, you will be free to decide the extent to which you are willing to conform. While you risk giving a negative impression by breaking a rule, doing so will not necessarily be offensive. You may simply be viewed as eccentric or as having poor judgment.

No upper-class person engages in manual labor in front of others. Arabs are surprised when they see Westerners washing their cars or sweeping the sidewalk. While upper-class Arabs may do some menial chores inside their homes, they do not do them in public or in front of others.

A white-collar or desk job in an office is much desired by Arabs because of the status it confers. There is an enormous difference between working with the hands and working as a clerk. Arabs who have white-collar jobs will resent being asked to do something they consider beneath their status. If, in an office situation, your requests are not being carried out, you may find that you have been asking a person to do something that is demeaning or threatening to his or her dignity. And not wishing to offend you, the employee would be hesitant to tell you.

An Egyptian interpreter in an American-managed hospital once told me that she was insulted when a Western doctor asked her to bring him a glass of water. She felt that her dignity had been threatened and that she had been treated like the "tea boy" who took orders for drinks.

Manual work is acceptable if it can be classified as a hobby—for example, sewing, painting, or craftwork. Refinishing furniture might get by as a hobby (though it would probably raise eyebrows), but repairing cars is out. If you decide to paint the exterior of your house or to refinish the floors yourself, expect to be the subject of conversation.

Upper-class Arabs are careful about their dress and appearance whenever they are in public, because the way a person dresses indicates his or her wealth and social standing. Arab children are often dressed in expensive clothes, and women wear a lot of jewelry, especially gold. The men are partial to expensive watches, cuff links, pens, and cigarette lighters. Looking their best and dressing well are essential to Arabs' self-respect, and they are surprised when they see well-to-do foreigners wearing casual or old clothes (faded jeans, a tattered T-shirt). Why would a person dress poorly when he or she can afford better?

Usually upper-class Arabs do not socialize with people from other classes, at least not in each other's homes. They may enjoy cordial relations with the corner grocer and newsstand vendor, but, like most Westerners, they would not suggest a dinner or an evening's entertainment together. (A possible exception is a big occasion like the celebration of a wedding.)

When you plan social events, do not mix people from different social classes. You can invite anyone from any class to your home, and the gesture will be much appreciated, but to invite a company director and your local baker at the same time would embarrass both parties.

Dealing with Service People

Westerners living in an Arab country usually have one or more household servants. You may feel free to establish a personal relationship with your servants; they appreciate the kindness and consideration they have come to expect from Westerners—"Please" and "Thank you" are never out of place. You may, in fact, work right alongside the servant, but you will notice that the relationship changes if Arab guests are present. The servant will then want to do all the work alone so as not to tarnish your social image. If a glass of water is spilled, for example, you should call the servant to clean up, rather than be seen doing it yourself. Inviting your servant to join you and your guests at tea or at a meal would be inappropriate and very embarrassing for everyone.

Servants expect you to assume some responsibility for them; you may, for example, be asked to pay medical expenses and to help out financially in family emergencies. Give at least something as a token of concern, then ask around to find out how much is reasonable for the situation. If you feel that the expense is too high for you to cover completely, you can offer to lend the money and deduct it from the person's salary over a period of time. Be generous with surplus food and with household items or clothing you no longer need, and remember that extra money is expected on holidays.

Make the acquaintance of shopkeepers, doormen, and er-
rand boys. Such acquaintances are best made by exchanging
a few words of Arabic and showing them that you like and
respect them.

If you become friendly with people who have relatively
little money, limit the frequency of your social visits. They
may be obliged to spend more than they can afford to receive
you properly, and the problem is far too embarrassing to
discuss or even admit. It is enjoyable to visit villagers or the
home of a taxi driver or shopkeeper, but if you plan to make
it a habit, bring gifts with you or find other ways to compen-
sate your hosts.

8

∧

The Role of the Family

Arab society is built around the extended family system. Individuals feel a strong affiliation with all of their relatives—aunts, uncles, and cousins—not just with their immediate family. The degree to which all blood relationships are encompassed by a family unit varies among families, but most Arabs have over a hundred "fairly close" relatives.

Family Loyalty and Obligations

Family loyalty and obligations take precedence over loyalty to friends or the demands of a job. Relatives are expected to help each other, including giving financial assistance if necessary.

Family affiliation provides security and assures one that he or she will never be entirely without resources, emotional or material. Only the most rash or foolhardy person would risk being censured or disowned by his or her family. Family support is indispensable in an unpredictable world; the family is a person's ultimate refuge.

Members of a family are expected to support each other in disputes with outsiders. Regardless of personal antipathy among relatives, they must defend each other's honor, counter criticism, and display group cohesion, if only for the sake of appearances. Internal family disputes rarely get to the point of open, public conflict.

Membership in a well-known and influential family ensures social acceptance and is often crucial to members in obtaining a good education, finding a good job, or succeeding in business. Arabs are very proud of their family connections and lineage.

The reputation of any member of a family group reflects on all of the other members. One person's indiscreet behavior or poor judgment can damage his or her relatives' pride, social influence, and marriage opportunities. For this reason family honor is the greatest source of pressure on an individual to conform to accepted behavior patterns, and one is constantly reminded of his or her responsibility for upholding that honor.

An employer must be understanding if an employee is late or absent because of family obligations. *It is unreasonable to expect an Arab employee to give priority to the demands of a job if they conflict with family duties.*

The description of Syrian society found in the book *Syria: A Country Study*, is applicable to Arab societies in general.

> Syrians highly value family solidarity and, consequently, obedience of children to the wishes of their parents. Being a good family member includes automatic loyalty to kinsmen as well. Syrians employed in modern bureaucratic positions, such as government officials, therefore find impersonal impartiality difficult to attain because of a conflict with the deeply held value of family solidarity.
>
> There is no similarly ingrained feeling of duty toward a job, an employer, a coworker, or even a friend. A widespread conviction exists that the only reliable people are one's kinsmen. An officeholder tends to select his kinsmen as fellow workers or subordinates because of a sense of responsibility for them and because of the feeling of trust between them. Commercial establishments are largely family operations staffed by the offspring and relatives of the owner. Cooperation among business firms may be determined by the presence

or absence of kinship ties between the heads of firms. When two young men become very close friends, they often enhance their relationship by accepting one another as "brothers," thus placing each in a position of special responsibility toward the other. There is no real basis for a close relationship except ties of kinship. (Collelo 1988, 82)

A particularly revealing interview with two brothers working at the Helwan steel mill in Egypt and living with several other brothers included the following exchange (inflation has greatly changed the value of money mentioned here).

"I only earn £2 a month," said one brother..."and this I give to my eldest brother. He takes it and buys food...if I need anything extra I ask him and he will get it for me."

"Yes," the eldest said to us. "That's the way it is. I earn £25 a month and I support all of them...they have no work so I have to."

"And what do you hope to gain?" we asked him.

"Nothing," he answered. "Only I hope they will get on, achieve something with their lives.... I know that if I then fall on hard times, they will not forsake me." (Thomas and Deakin 1975, 99)

Relations among Family Members

An Arab man is recognized as the head of his immediate family, and his role and influence are overt. His wife also has a clearly defined sphere of influence, but it exists largely behind the scenes. Although an Arab woman is careful to show deference to her husband in public, she may not always accord him the same submissiveness in private.

In matters where opinions among family members differ, much consultation and negotiation take place before decisions are made. If a compromise cannot be reached, however, the husband, father, or older men in the family prevail.

Status in a family increases as a person grows older, and most families have patriarchs or matriarchs whose opinions are given considerable weight in family matters. Children are taught profound respect for adults, a pattern that is pervasive in Arab society at all ages. It is common, for example, for adults to refrain from smoking in front of their parents or older relatives.

Responsibility for other members of the family rests heavily on older men in the extended family and on older sons in the immediate family. Children are their parents' "social security," and grown sons, in particular, are responsible for the support of their parents. In the absence of the father, brothers are responsible for their unmarried sisters.

Members of a family are very dependent on each other emotionally, and these ties continue throughout a person's life. Some people feel closer to their brothers and sisters and confide in them more than they do their spouses. Edward T. Hall, in *The Hidden Dimension*, comments on this interdependence as it relates to the allocation of space in Arab homes:

> Arab spaces inside their upper middle-class homes are tremendous by our standards. They avoid partitions because Arabs do not like to be alone. The form of the home is such as to hold the family together inside a single protective shell, because Arabs are deeply involved with each other. Their personalities are intermingled and take nourishment from each other like the roots and soil. If one is not with people and actively involved in some way, one is deprived of life. An old Arab saying reflects this value: "Paradise without people should not be entered because it is Hell." (1966, 5)

In the traditional Arab family, the roles of the mother and the father are quite different as they relate to their children. The mother is seen as a source of emotional support and steadfast loving-kindness. She is patient, forgiving, and prone to indulge and spoil her children, especially her sons. The father, while seen as a source of love, may display affection less overtly; he is also the source of authority and punish-ment. Some Arab fathers feel that their status in the family is best maintained by cultivating awe and even a degree of fear in other members of the family.

In most Arab families the parents maintain very close contact with their own parents and with their brothers and sisters. For this reason Arab children grow up experiencing constant interaction with older relatives, especially their grandparents, who often live in the same home. This contrib-utes to the passing on of social values from one generation to another, as the influence of the older relatives is continually present. Relatively few Arab teenagers and young adults rebel against family values and desires, certainly not to the extent common in Western societies. Even people who affect mod-ern tastes in dress, reading material, and entertainment sub-scribe to prevailing social values and expect their own family lives to be very similar to that of their parents.

Marriage

Most Arabs still prefer family-arranged marriages. Though marriage customs are changing in some modern circles, couples still seek family approval of the person they have chosen. This is essential as an act of respect toward their parents, and people rarely marry in defiance of their families.

Arabs feel that because marriage is such a major decision, it is considered prudent to leave it to the family's discretion rather than to choose someone solely on the basis of emotion or ideas of romance. In almost all Arab countries and social groups, however, the prospective bride and bridegroom have the opportunity to meet, visit, and become acquainted—and even to accept or reject a proposal of marriage. The degree to which the individuals are consulted will vary according to how traditional or modern the family is.

Among Muslim Arabs, especially in rural and nomadic communities, the preferred pattern of marriage is to a first or second cousin. In fact, marriage to relatives is on the rise. In 1996, 58 percent of Iraq's citizens still married their cousins, followed by Saudi Arabia with 55 percent, then Kuwait and Jordan with 54 percent and 50 percent, respectively ("Kissing Cousins" 1996, 9). Since an important part of a marriage arrangement is the investigation into the social and financial standing of the proposed candidates, it is reassuring to marry someone whose background, character, and financial position are well known. Marriage to a cousin also ensures that money, in the form of a dowry or inheritance, stays within the family.

In contrast with Western customs, Arab couples do not enter marriage with idealistic or romantic expectations. True, they are seeking companionship and love, but equally important, they want financial security, social status, and children. These goals are realistic and are usually attained. Arab marriages are, on the whole, very stable and characterized by mutual respect. Having a happy family life is considered an important goal in the Arab World.

Divorce

Most Arab Christians belong to denominations which do not permit divorce. Among Muslims, divorce is permitted and carefully regulated by religious law.

Divorce is common enough that it does not carry a social stigma for the individuals involved, and people who have been divorced are eligible for remarriage. There is probably not as much personal pain associated with divorce if the marriage was arranged; obtaining a divorce is not an admission of mistaken judgment or an implied statement of personal failure, as it is sometimes viewed in Western society.

Although a Muslim man may divorce his wife if he wishes, he risks severe damage to his social image if he is arbitrary or hasty about his decision. The process is quite simple: he merely recites the formula for divorce ("I divorce you") in front of witnesses. If he says the formula once or twice, the couple can still be reconciled; if he repeats it a third time, it is binding. A woman has more difficulty in initiating divorce proceedings, but usually she is successful on grounds of childlessness, desertion, or nonsupport. A woman must go through court proceedings in order to divorce her husband. In Jordan, Syria, and Morocco, she may write into her marriage contract the right to initiate divorce (Anderson 1976, 116). Some Arab countries now require a man to go through court proceedings as well.

When a Muslim woman is divorced, her husband must pay a divorce settlement, which is included in every marriage contract and is usually a very large sum of money. In addition she is entitled to financial support for herself for at least three months (a waiting period to determine that she is not pregnant) and more if she needs it, as well as support for her minor children while they are in her custody. Additional conditions can be written into a marriage contract.

Some Arab countries follow Islamic law entirely in matters of divorce; others have supplemented it. Laws pertaining to divorce have been widely discussed, and changes are constantly being proposed. For example, the custody of children is theoretically determined by Islamic law. They are to stay with their mothers to a certain age (approximately seven years for boys and nine years for girls, though it differs slightly among countries), and then they may go to their fathers. This shift is not always automatic, however, and may be ruled upon by a court or religious judge, according to the circumstances of the case.

Child-Rearing Practices

Arabs dearly love children, and both men and women express that love openly. Arab children grow up surrounded by adoring relatives who share in child rearing by feeding, caring for, and even disciplining each other's children. Because so many people have cared for them and served as authority figures and because the practice is so universal, Arabs are remarkably homogeneous in their experience of childhood. Arab children learn the same values in much the same way; their upbringing is not as arbitrarily dependent on the approach of their particular parents as it is in Western societies.

In traditional Arab culture there has always been a marked preference for boys over girls because men contribute more to the family's influence in the community. Arab children are provided different role models for personality development. Boys are expected to be aggressive and decisive; girls are expected to be more passive. This attitude toward boys and girls is starting to change now that women are being educated and becoming wage earners. Many Arab couples practice birth control and limit the size of their families to two or three children, even if they are all girls.

Some educated or liberal-thinking Arabs find the pressure from the family to conform to rigid social standards to be oppressive. Much of what has been written on the subject of Arab character and personality development is extremely negative, particularly statements made by Arabs themselves.* Clearly many Arabs feel resentful of the requirements imposed by their families and by society and believe that conformity leads to the development of undesirable personal traits. Sania Hamady makes this point emphatically, perhaps too categorically.

> He [the Arab] is tied hand and foot by the demands and interference of his group. He is not left alone to do what he pleases. His duties, if not fulfilled, are exacted from him. Advice is given even when not asked for.... He may not make decisions for himself without consulting his near relatives and the senior members of his group. (1960, 32)

---

* See, for example, the description of child-rearing practices in Sharabi and Ani (1977), 240–56, or almost anywhere in Hamady (1960).

Most Arabs feel that while their childhood was, in many ways, a time of stringent demands, it was also a time of indulgence and openly expressed love, especially from their mothers. Failure to conform is punished, but methods of discipline are usually not harsh.

In Arab culture the most important requirement for a "good" child is respectful behavior in front of adults. Children must greet adults with a handshake, stay to converse for a few minutes if asked, and refrain from interrupting or talking back. Children often help to serve guests and thus learn the requirements of hospitality early. Westerners who want their children to make a good impression on Arab guests might wish to keep these customs in mind.

Among Arabs it is an extremely important responsibility to bring children up so that they will reflect well on the family. It is an insult to accuse someone of not being well raised. Children's character and success in life reflect directly on their parents. Arabs tend to give parents much of the credit for their children's successes and much of the blame for their failures. Parents readily make sacrifices for their children's welfare; they expect these efforts to be acknowledged and their parental influence to continue throughout the child's lifetime.

Many Western parents begin training their children at an early age to become independent and self-reliant. They give the children token jobs and regular allowance money and frequently encourage them to make their own decisions. This training helps children avoid being dependent on their parents after they have reached adulthood.

Arab parents, on the other hand, welcome their children's dependence. Mothers, especially, try to keep their children tied to them emotionally. Young people continue to live at home until they are married and then, at least in traditional families, young married couples live with the husband's parents. It is customary for the parents of a newly married couple to furnish the couple's home entirely and to continue to help them financially.

Talking about Your Family

Given this emphasis on family background and honor, you may want to carefully consider the impression you will make when giving information to Arabs about your family relationships. Saying the wrong thing can affect your image and status.

Arabs are very surprised if someone talks about poverty and disadvantages experienced in early life. Rather than admiring one's success in overcoming such circumstances, they wonder why anyone would admit to humble origins when it need not be known.

If your father held a low-status job; if you have relatives, especially female relatives, who have disgraced the family; or if you have elderly relatives in a nursing home (which Arabs find shocking), there is nothing to be gained by talking about it. If you dislike your parents or any close relatives, keep your thoughts to yourself. On the other hand, if you are from a prominent family or are related to a well-known person, letting people know this information can work to your advantage.

In sum, if you do not have positive things to say about your family, things that will incline Arabs to admiration, it is best to avoid the subject.

9

Religion and Society

Arabs identify strongly with their religious groups, whether they are Muslim or Christian and whether they participate in religious observances or not. A foreigner must be aware of the pervasive role of religion in Arab life in order to avoid causing offense by injudicious statements or actions.

Religious Affiliation

Religious affiliation is essential for every person in Arab society. There is no place for an atheist or an agnostic. If you have no religious affiliation or are an atheist, this should not be mentioned. Shock and amazement would be the reaction of most Arabs, along with a loss of respect for you. Arabs place great value on piety and respect anyone who sincerely practices his or her religion, no matter what that religion is.

Religious Practices

An Arab's religion affects his or her whole way of life on a daily basis. Religion is taught in the schools, the language is full of religious expressions, and people practice their religion openly, almost obtrusively, expressing it in numerous ways: decorations on cars and in homes; jewelry in the form of gold crosses, miniature Qur'ans, or pendants inscribed with Qur'anic verses; and religious names.

"For an Arab Muslim of pious persuasion, his faith is more than a religion; it is a complete way of life, because Islam and the forces of society are in constant interplay. Islam is politics, law, social behavior..." (Lamb 1987, 15). It is significant that one of the most popular slogans among Islamists is simply: "Islam is the Solution."

Muslims say the Qur'anic formula, "In the name of God, the Merciful, the Compassionate" (*Bismillah Ar-Rahman Ar-Raheem*), whenever they are setting out on a trip, about to undertake a dangerous task, or beginning a speech. This formula is printed at the top of business letterheads and included at the beginning of reports and personal letters—it even appears on business receipts.

For both Muslims and Christians, marriage and divorce are controlled by religious law. In some countries there is no such thing as a civil marriage; it must be performed by a religious official. For Muslims inheritance is also controlled by religious law, and in conservative countries religious law partially determines methods of criminal punishment.

The practice of "Islamic banking" is gaining in popularity. The Islamic religion forbids lending money at a fixed rate of interest, viewing it as unfair and exploitative. Islamic banks, therefore, place investors' money in "shared risk" partnership accounts, with rates of return varying according to profits (or losses) on investments.

Marriage across religious lines is rare, although the Islamic religion permits a Muslim man to marry a Jewish or Christian woman without requiring that his wife convert. A Muslim woman, however, must marry a Muslim man; in this way the children are assured of being Muslim (children are considered to have the religion of their father).

Never make critical remarks about any religious practice. *In Arab culture all religions and their practices are treated with respect.*

If you are a Christian foreigner and ask Christian Arabs about accompanying them to church services, they will be very pleased. Non-Muslims do not attend Islamic religious services, however, and you should not enter a mosque until you have checked whether it is permitted, which varies from country to country and even from mosque to mosque.

The Religion of Islam

To understand Arab culture it is essential that you become familiar with Islamic history and doctrine. If you do, you will gain insights that few Westerners have, and your efforts will be greatly appreciated.

The Islamic religion had its origin in northern Arabia in the seventh century A.D. The doctrines of Islam are based on revelations from God to His last prophet, Muhammad, over a period of twenty-two years. The revelations were preserved and incorporated into the holy book of the Muslims, the Qur'an.*

The God Muslims worship is the same God Jews and Christians worship (*Allah* is simply the Arabic word for *God*). Islam is defined as a return to the faith of Abraham, the prophet who made a covenant with God.

The Qur'an contains doctrines that guide Muslims to correct behavior so that they will find salvation on the Day of Judgment, narrative stories illustrating God's benevolence and power, and social regulations for the Muslim community. It is the single most important guiding force for Muslims and touches on virtually every aspect of their lives.

The word *Islam* means "submission" (to the will of God), and *Muslim* (also spelled "Moslem," which is more familiar to Westerners but not as close to the Arabic pronunciation)

---

* The Qur'an is the most read, recited, memorized, debated, analyzed, and venerated book in the annals of history (Sardar 1994, 48).

means "one who submits." The doctrines of the Islamic religion are viewed as a summation and completion of previous revelations to Jewish and Christian prophets. Islam shares many doctrines with Judaism and Christianity, and Jews and Christians are known as "People of the Book" (the Scriptures).

Shortly after the advent of Islam, the Arabs began an energetic conquest of surrounding territory and eventually expanded their empire from Spain to India. The widespread conversion to Islam by the people in the Middle East and North Africa accounts for the fact that today over 90 percent of all Arabs are Muslims.

Most Muslim Arabs are *Sunni* (also called "orthodox"), and they constitute 85 percent of Muslims. Fifteen percent are *Shiite* and are found in Lebanon, Iraq, and the Arabian Gulf (Iran, the most important Shiite country, is not Arab). The separation of the Muslims into two groups stems from a dispute over the proper succession of authority (the "caliphate") after the death of the Prophet Muhammad. Sunnis and Shiites differ today in some of their religious practices and emphases on certain doctrines, but both groups recognize each other as Muslims.

Muslim society is governed by the Sharia, or Islamic law, which is based on the Qur'an and the *Sunnah*. The Sunnah is the description of the acts and sayings of the Prophet and incorporates the *Hadith* (traditions of the Prophet). Islamic jurists also use *ijma'* (consensus) and *qiyas* (reasoning by analogy) when interpreting and applying Islamic law.

The application of Islamic law differs by country and local interpretation of the Qur'an and Sharia law. Some countries (Saudi Arabia, Libya, Sudan) follow it almost exclusively in domestic and criminal law, but most have modified or supplemented it. Islamic jurists are faced with new issues on which there has not been final agreement. Birth control, for instance, which is permitted in most Islamic countries, is openly promoted by some and discouraged by others. Pakistan (a

Muslim, non-Arab country), for example, outlawed birth control on the basis of religious principles. There are many Islamic conferences where issues such as population control (Ammar 1995), women's dress, capital punishment, nuclear and biological warfare, terrorism, human rights, and societal pluralism are discussed. There is, however, no binding central authority to enforce agreed-upon decisions.

Currently there are approximately 1.3 billion Muslims in the world, of which one-fifth, or over two hundred million, are Arabs. Large Muslim populations also exist in Africa, the Indian subcontinent, and Southeast Asia.

The basic tenets of the Islamic faith are the five "pillars" (primary obligations) of Islam:

Reciting the Declaration of Faith ("There is no God but God and Muhammad is the Messenger [Prophet] of God"). The recitation of this declaration with sincere intention in front of two male Muslim witnesses is sufficient for a person to become a Muslim.

Arabs, Muslims and Christians alike, intersperse their ordinary conversations with references to the will of God (see "Social Greetings," Appendix C). To make a good impression, you are advised to do the same. Using Arabic religious expressions acts as a formal acknowledgment of the importance of religious faith in their society.

Praying five times daily. The five prayers are dawn, noon, afternoon, sunset, and night, and their times differ slightly every day. Muslims are reminded of prayer through a "prayer call" broadcast from the minaret of a mosque. A Muslim prays facing in the direction of the Kaaba in Mecca. The weekly communal prayer service is the noon prayer in the mosque on Fridays, generally attended by men (women may go but it is not as common, nor is it expected). The Friday prayer also includes a sermon. Prayer is regulated by ritual purification beforehand and a predetermined number of prostrations and recitations, depending on the time of day. The prayer ritual includes standing, bowing, touching the forehead to the floor (which is covered with a prayer mat, rug, or other clean surface), sitting back, and holding the hands in cupped position. Muslims may pray in a mosque, in their home or office, or in public places.

Avoid staring at, walking in front of, or interrupting a person during prayer.

The Call to Prayer, broadcast from minarets five times a day, contains the following phrases, the repetition of which varies slightly depending on the time of day:

God is Great.

I testify that there is no god but God.

I testify that Muhammad is God's messenger.

Come to prayer.

Come to success.

God is Great.

There is no god but God.

If you learn the Call in Arabic, it will add to your pleasure in hearing it (many Westerners become so accustomed to the Call that they miss it when they leave). The first statement, *Allahu Akbar* (God is Great), is much used in Islam in other contexts as well. It is, in fact, "the dominant cultural chord of Islam, the declaration that punctuates all life, the reason to believe, the motive for action, inspiration for soldier and revolutionary, consolation for the oppressed" (Lippman 1990, 13).

Giving alms (charity) to the needy. Muslims are required to give as *Zakat* (a religious tax) $2^1/_2$ percent of their net annual income (after basic family expenses) for the welfare of the community in general and for the poor in particular. Some people assess themselves annually and give the money to a government or community entity; others distribute charity throughout the year.

If you are asked for alms by a beggar, it is best to give a token amount. Even if you give nothing, avoid saying no, which is very rude. Instead, say *"Allah ya'teek"* (God give you); at least you have given the person a blessing.

Fasting during the month of Ramadan. Ramadan is the ninth

month of the Islamic lunar calendar (which is eleven days short, so religious holidays move forward every year). During Ramadan, Muslims do not eat, drink, or smoke between sunrise and sunset. The purpose of fasting is to experience hunger and deprivation and to perform an act of self-discipline, humility, and faith. The Ramadan fast is not required of persons whose health may be endangered, and travelers are also excused; however, anyone who is excused must make up the missed fast days later when health and circumstances permit. In most communities, Ramadan brings with it a holiday atmosphere, as people gather with family and friends to break the fast at elaborate meals. Work hours are shortened, shops change their opening and closing hours, and most activities take place in the early morning or late at night.

Be considerate of people who are fasting during Ramadan by refraining from eating, drinking, or smoking in public places during the fasting hours. To express good wishes to someone before or during Ramadan, you say *Ramadan Kareem* (Gracious Ramadan), to which the response is *Allahu Akram* (God is more gracious).

Performing a pilgrimage to Mecca at least once during one's lifetime if finances permit. The Hajj is the peak religious experience for many Muslims. In the twelfth month of the Islamic year, Muslims from all over the world gather in Saudi Arabia to perform several separate activities, which are carried out at different sites in the Mecca and Medina area over a period of six days. The Hajj commemorates the patriarch Abraham. Pilgrims, men and women, wear white garments to symbolize their state of purity and their equality in the sight of God. At the end of the Hajj period is a holiday during which all families who can afford it sacrifice a sheep (or other animal) and, after taking enough for one meal, share the rest of it with the poor. Sharing on this holiday is such an important gesture that each year many governments send surplus sacrificial meat to refugees and to the poor in countries such as Sudan, Pakistan, and Chad.

When someone is departing for the pilgrimage, the appropriate blessing is *Hajj Mabroor* (Reverent Pilgrimage). When someone returns, offer congratulations and add the title *Hajj* (*Hajja* for a woman) to the person's name (except in Saudi Arabia, where the title is not used).

The Qur'an and the Bible

Much of the content of the Qur'an is similar (though not identical) to the teachings and stories found in the Old and New Testaments of the Bible. Islamic doctrine accepts the previous revelations to biblical prophets as valid, but states, as the Bible does, that the people continually strayed from these teachings. Correct guidance had to be repeated through different prophets, one after the other. By the seventh century, doctrines and practices again had to be corrected through the revelations to Muhammad, who is known as the last, or "seal," of the prophets.

The Qur'an is divided into 114 chapters, arranged in order of length, longest to shortest (with a few exceptions). The chapters are not in chronological order, although the reader can identify whether a chapter was revealed in Mecca (earlier) or Medina (later). Each chapter is made up of verses. If you decide to read the Qur'an in translation, it is a good idea to obtain a list of the chapters in chronological order and read through them in that order so that the development of thought and teachings becomes clear.†

Most of the chapters in the Qur'an are in cadenced, rhymed verse, while some (particularly the later Medinan ones) are in prose. The sustained rhythm of the recited Qur'an, combined

---

† A list of Qur'anic chapters in chronological order may be found in Richard Bell's *Introduction to the Qur'an* (1953). The 1964 edition of the translation of the Qur'an by N. J. Dawood also presents the chapters in chronological rather than traditional order (this was changed in later editions).

with the beauty of its content, accounts for its great esthetic and poetic effect when heard in Arabic. The Qur'an is considered the epitome of Arabic writing style, and when it is recited aloud, it can move listeners to tears. The elegance and beauty of the Qur'an taken as proof of its divine origin—no human being could expect to reproduce it successfully.

The three most often cited characteristics of the Qur'an are these: it is inimitable, it is eternal (it always existed but was not manifested until the seventh century), and it is in Arabic (the Arabic version is the direct Word of God, so translations of the Qur'an into other languages are not used for prayer).

It is common for Muslims to memorize the Qur'an, or large portions of it; a person who can recite the Qur'an is called a *hafiz*. Reading and reciting the Qur'an was once the traditional form of education, and often the only education many people received. In most Arab schools today memorization of Qur'anic passages is included in the curriculum. The word *Qur'an* means "recitation" in Arabic.

The Qur'an and the Bible have much in common:

• the necessity of faith

• reward for good actions and punishment for evil actions on the Day of Judgment

• the concept of Heaven (Paradise) and Hell

• the existence of angels who communicate between God and man

• the existence of Satan (*Shaytan* in Arabic)

• the recognition of numerous prophets.[‡]

[‡] The Qur'an recognizes eighteen Old Testament figures as prophets (among them Adam, Noah, Abraham, Ishmael, Isaac, Jacob, Moses, Joseph, Job) and three New Testament figures (Zachariah, John the Baptist, and Jesus), and it mentions four prophets who do not appear in the Bible. Of all these prophets, five are considered the most important. In order of chronology these are: Noah, Abraham, Moses, Jesus, and Muhammad.

- the prohibition of the consumption of pork and the flesh of animals not slaughtered in a ritual manner, which is very similar to kosher dietary law in the Old Testament

- the teaching that Jesus was born of a virgin. Mary is called "Miriam" in Arabic (the theme is the same, although details differ)

- the teaching that Jesus worked miracles, including curing the sick and raising the dead

There are some notable differences between the Qur'an and the Bible as well.

- Islam does not recognize the concept of intercession between God and man; all prayers must be made to God directly. Jesus is recognized as one of the most important prophets, but the Christian concept of his intercession for man's sins is not accepted.

- Islam teaches that Jesus was not crucified; instead, a person made to look like him was miraculously substituted in his place on the cross. God would not allow such an event to happen to one of His prophets.

- Islam does not accept the doctrine of Jesus' resurrection and divinity.

- Islam is uncompromisingly monotheistic and rejects the Christian concept of the Trinity.

Some of the biblical stories that are retold in the Qur'an (in a shortened version) include the following:

- the story of the Creation
- the story of Adam and Eve
- the story of Cain and Abel
- the story of Noah and the Flood

- the story of the covenant of Abraham and his willingness to sacrifice his son as a test of faith.§
- the story of Lot and the destruction of the evil cities
- the story of Joseph (told in much detail)
- the story of David and Goliath
- the story of Solomon and the Queen of Sheba
- the story of the afflictions of Job
- the story of the birth of Jesus.‖

Muslims feel an affinity with the Jewish and Christian religions and find it unfortunate that so few Westerners understand how similar the Islamic religion is to their own. Islam is a continuation of the other two religions, and Muslims view it as the one true faith.

Passages from the Qur'an

Selected passages from the Qur'an are presented here to give the reader an idea of the tone and content of the book (from *The Koran Interpreted,* by A. J. Arberry, 1955). Titles of chapters refer to key words in that chapter, not to content.

---

§ Islam holds that he was ordered to sacrifice Ishmael, whereas the Bible states that it was Isaac. Abraham is recognized as the ancestor of the Arabs through Ishmael.

‖ In the Qur'anic version, Jesus was born at the foot of a palm tree in the desert and saved his unmarried mother from scorn when, as an infant, he spoke up in her defense and declared himself a prophet, saying "...Peace be upon me, the day I was born, and the day I die, and the day I am raised up alive" (referring to his resurrection on the Day of Judgment). This is a miracle of Jesus not recorded in the Bible.

Chapter 1: The Opening

In the Name of God, the Merciful, the Compassionate.
Praise belongs to God, the Lord of all Being
the All-merciful, the All-compassionate
the Master of the Day of Doom.

Thee only we serve; to Thee alone we pray for succour.
Guide us in the straight path,
the path of those whom Thou hast blessed,
not of those against whom Thou art wrathful,
nor of those who are astray.

Chapter 5: The Table

(Verse 3)
Today the unbelievers have despaired of
your religion; therefore fear them not,
but fear you Me.

Today I have perfected your religion
for you, and I have completed My blessing
upon you, and I have approved Islam for
your religion.

(Verse 120)
To God belongs the kingdom of the heavens
and of the earth, and all that is in them,
and He is powerful over everything.

Chapter 93: The Forenoon

(This chapter begins with an oath, which is common in the
Qur'an.)
In the Name of God, the Merciful, the Compassionate.
By the white forenoon
  and the brooding night!

Thy Lord has neither forsaken thee nor hates thee
  and the Last [life] shall be better for thee than the First.
Thy Lord shall give thee, and thou shalt be satisfied.

Did He not find thee an orphan, and shelter thee?
Did He not find thee erring, and guide thee?
Did He not find thee needy, and suffice thee?

As for the orphan, do not oppress him,
  and as for the beggar, scold him not;
  and as for thy Lord's blessing, declare it.

Communicating with Arabs

This chapter is about the Arabic language. Though you may never learn Arabic, you will need to know something about the language and how it is used.

Arabic is the native language of 220 million people and the official language of some twenty countries. In 1973 it was named the sixth official language of the United Nations, and it is the fourth most widely spoken language in the world. Only Mandarin Chinese, English, and Spanish have more speakers (*Merriam-Webster's Collegiate Dictionary* 1993, 673).

Arabic originated as one of the northern Semitic languages. The only other Semitic languages still in wide use today are Hebrew (revived as a spoken language only in this century) and Amharic (Ethiopian), which is from the southern Semitic branch. There are still a few speakers of the other northern Semitic languages (Aramaic, Syriac, and Chaldean) in Lebanon, Syria, and Iraq.

Many English words have been borrowed from Arabic, the most easily recognizable being those that begin with *al* (the Arabic word for "the"), such as *algebra, alchemy, alcove, alcohol,* and *alkali.* Many pertain to mathematics and the sciences; medieval European scholars drew heavily on Arabic source materials in these fields. Other Arabic words include

cipher, azimuth, algorithm, and *almanac.* Some foods that originated in the East brought their Arabic names west with
them—*coffee, sherbet, sesame, apricot, ginger, saffron,* and
carob.*

Varieties of Arabic

Spoken Arabic in all its forms is very different from written
Arabic. The written version is Classical Arabic, the language
that was in use in the seventh century A.D., in the Hejaz area
of Arabia. It is this rich, poetic language of the Qur'an that
has persisted as the written language of all Arabic-speaking
peoples since that time. Classical Arabic, which has evolved
into Modern Standard Arabic to accommodate new words
and usages, is sacred to the Arabs, esthetically pleasing, and
far more grammatically complex than the spoken or colloquial dialects.

The spoken languages are Formal Spoken Arabic and colloquial Arabic; the latter includes many dialects and
subdialects. Although some of them differ from each other as
much as Spanish does from Italian or the Scandinavian languages do from each other, they are all recognized as Arabic.
When Arabic spread throughout the Middle East and North
Africa with the Arab conquests, it mixed with and assimi-
lated local languages, spawning the dialects which are spoken
today.

An overview of Arabic language usage reveals the following:

1. *Classical (Modern Standard) Arabic.* Classical Arabic is
   used for all writing and for formal discussions, speeches,
   and news broadcasts but not for ordinary conversation. It
   is the same in all Arab countries, except for occasional
   variations in regional or specialized vocabulary.

---

* For more examples see Munir Al-Ba'albaki (1982), 101–12.

2. *Colloquial Arabic (dialects).* Colloquial Arabic is used for everyday spoken communication but not for writing, except sometimes in very informal correspondence, in film or play scripts, or as slang in cartoons and the like.

3. *Formal Spoken Arabic.* Formal Spoken Arabic is improvised, consisting principally of Classical Arabic terminology within the structure of the local dialect; it is used by educated people when they converse with Arabs whose dialect is very different from their own.

The Superiority of Arabic

Arabs are secure in the knowledge that their language is superior to all others. This attitude about one's own language is held by many people in the world, but in the case of the Arabs, they can point to several factors as proof of their assertion.

Most important, when the Qur'an was revealed directly from God, Arabic was the medium chosen for His message; its use was not an accident. Arabic is also extremely difficult to master, and it is complex grammatically; this is viewed as another sign of superiority. Because its structure lends itself to rhythm and rhyme, Arabic is pleasing to listen to when recited aloud. Finally, it has an unusually large vocabulary and its grammar allows for the easy coining of new words, so that borrowing from other languages is less common in Arabic than in many other languages. In other words, Arabic is richer than other languages, or so it is argued.

While most Westerners feel an affection for their native language, the pride and love Arabs feel for Arabic are much more intense. The Arabic language is their greatest cultural treasure and achievement, an art form that unfortunately cannot be accessed or appreciated by outsiders.

The Prestige of Classical Arabic

The reverence for Arabic pertains only to Classical Arabic, which is what Arabs mean by the phrase "the Arabic language." This was illustrated by the comment of an Egyptian village headman who once explained to me why he considered the village school to be important. "For one thing," he said, "that's where the children go to learn Arabic."

To the contrary, Arabic dialects have no prestige. Some people go so far as to suggest that they have "no grammar" and are not worthy of serious study. Committees of scholars have coined new words and tried to impose conventional usages to partially replace the dialects, but they have had no more success than language regulatory groups in other countries.

A good command of Classical Arabic is highly admired in the Arab culture because it is difficult to attain. Few people other than scholars and specialists in Arabic have enough confidence to speak extemporaneously in Classical Arabic or to defend their written style.

To become truly literate in Arabic requires more years of study than are required for English literacy. The student must learn new words in Classical Arabic (more than 50 percent of the words are different from the local dialect in some countries)[†] and a whole new grammar, including case endings and new verb forms. The literacy problem in the Arab World stems significantly from the difficulty of Classical Arabic. Even people who have had five or six years of schooling are still considered functionally illiterate (unable to use the writ-

---

[†] A study was conducted in Tunisia in the early 1970s, comparing the vocabulary of six-year-old Tunisian children with equivalent vocabulary in Modern Standard Arabic, the medium through which they would be taught to read. It was found that over 70 percent of the vocabulary words were different (information from personal communication with professors, University of Tunis).

ten language for anything more than rudimentary needs, such as signing one's name or reading signs).

From time to time Arab scholars have suggested that Classical Arabic be replaced by written dialects to facilitate education and literacy. This idea has been repeatedly and emphatically denounced by the large majority of Arabs and has almost no chance of acceptance in the foreseeable future. The most serious objection is that Classical Arabic is the language of the Qur'an. Another argument is that if it were supplanted by the dialects, the entire body of Arabic literature and poetry would become unattainable, and if translated into a dialect, it would lose much of its beauty.

There is a political argument too. Classical Arabic is a cultural force that unites all Arabs. To discard it, many fear, would lead to a linguistic fragmentation which would exacerbate the tendencies toward political and psychological fragmentation already present.

Eloquence of Speech

Eloquence is emphasized and admired in the Arab World far more than in the West, which accounts for the "flowery" prose in Arabic, in both written and spoken form. *Instead of viewing rhetoric in a disparaging way, as Westerners often do, Arabs admire it.* The ability to speak eloquently is a sign of education and refinement.

Foreign observers frequently comment on long-winded political speeches and the repetition of phrases and themes in Arabic, failing to understand that the speaker's style of delivery and command of the language appeal to the listeners as much as does the message itself. Exaggerations, threats, promises, and nationalistic slogans are meant more for momentary effect than as statements of policy or belief, yet foreigners too often take them literally, especially when encountered in the cold light of a foreign language translation. *In the Arab World how you say something is as important as what you have to say.*

Eloquence is a clue to the popular appeal of some nationalistic leaders whose words are far more compelling than their deeds. Much of the personal charisma attributed to them is due in large part to their ability to speak in well-phrased, rhetorical Arabic. This was true of the late Gamal Abdel Nasser, for example, and is true of Muammar Qaddhafi today.

Arabs devote considerable effort to using their language creatively and effectively. As Leslie J. McLoughlin, an Arabic specialist, says,

> Westerners are not in everyday speech given, as Arabs are, to quoting poetry, ancient proverbs and extracts from holy books. Nor are they wont to exchange fulsome greetings.... Perhaps the greatest difference between the Levantine approach to language and that of Westerners is that Levantines, like most Arabs, take pleasure in using language for its own sake. The *sahra* (or evening entertainment) may well take the form of talk alone, but talk of a kind forgotten in the West except in isolated communities such as Irish villages or Swiss mountain communities—talk not merely comical, tragical, historical/pastoral, etc., but talk ranging over poetry, story telling, anecdotes, jokes, word games, singing and acting. (1982, 2–3)

Speech Mannerisms

Making yourself completely understood by another person is a difficult task under the best of circumstances. It is more difficult still if you each have dramatically different ways of expressing yourself. Such is the problem between Westerners and Arabs, which often results in misunderstanding, leaving both parties feeling bewildered or deceived.

Arabs talk a lot, repeat themselves, shout when excited, and make extensive use of gestures. They punctuate their conversations with oaths (such as "I swear by God") to emphasize what they say, and they exaggerate for effect. Foreigners sometimes wonder if they are involved in a discussion or an argument.

If you speak softly and make your statements only once, Arabs may wonder if you really mean what you are saying. People will ask, "Do you really mean that?" or "Is that true?" It's not that they do not believe you, but they need repetition and a few emphatic "yeses" to be reassured.

Arabs have a great tolerance for noise and interference during discussions; often several people speak at once (each trying to outshout the other), interspersing their statements with table pounding and threatening (or playful) gestures, all the while being coached by bystanders. Businessmen interrupt meetings to greet callers, answer the telephone, and sign papers brought in by clerks. A foreigner may feel that he or she can be heard only by insisting on the precondition of being allowed to speak without interruption. *Loudness of speech is mainly for dramatic effect and in most cases should not be taken as an indication of how strongly the speaker feels about what he or she is saying.*

In a taxi in Cairo once, my driver was shouting and complaining and gesticulating wildly to other drivers as he worked his way through the crowded streets. In the midst of all this action, he turned around, laughed, and winked. "You know," he said, "sometimes I really enjoy this!"

Some situations absolutely demand emotion and drama. In Baghdad I was in a taxi when it was hit from the rear. Both drivers leaped out of their cars and began shouting at each other. After waiting ten minutes, while a crowd gathered, I decided to pay the fare and leave. I pushed through the crowd and got the driver's attention. He broke off the argument, politely told me that there was nothing to pay, and then resumed the argument at full voice.

Loud and boisterous behavior does have limits, however. It is more frequent, of course, among people of approximately the same age and social status who know each other well. It occurs mostly in social situations, less often in business meetings, and is not acceptable when dealing with elders or social superiors, in which case polite deference is required. Bedouins and the Arabs of Saudi Arabia and the Gulf tend to be more reserved and soft-spoken, at least in more or less formal discussions. In fact, *in almost every respect, protocol is stricter in the Arabian Peninsula* than elsewhere in the Arab World.

The Power of Words

To the Arab way of thinking (consciously or subconsciously), words have power; they can, to some extent, affect subsequent events. Arab conversation is peppered with blessings, which are like little prayers for good fortune, intended to help keep things going well. *Swearing and the use of curses and obscenities is very offensive to Arabs.* If words have power and can affect events, it is feared that curses may bring misfortune just by being uttered.

The liberal use of blessings also demonstrates that the speaker holds no envy toward a person or object; in other words, that he or she does not cast an "evil eye" toward something. Belief in the evil eye (often just called "the eye") is common, and it is feared or acknowledged to some extent by most Arabs, although less so by the better educated. It is widely believed that a person or object can be harmed if viewed (even unconsciously) with envy—with an evil eye. The harm may be prevented, however, by offering blessings or statements of goodwill. Even foreigners who do not know about the evil eye may be suspected of giving it. When a Jordanian proudly showed his new car to a British friend, the latter said, "It's beautiful! I wish I could afford a car like that!" Two weeks later the Jordanian had a serious car accident. When his British friend paid him a visit, the Jordanian received him coolly and their friendship never revived. The Briton now believes that it was his inadvertent expression of apparent envy that destroyed the friendship.

Euphemisms

Arabs are uncomfortable discussing illness, disaster, or death. This trait illustrates how the power of words affects Arab speech and behavior. *A careless reference to bad events can lead to misfortune or make a bad situation worse.* Arabs avoid such references as much as possible and use euphemisms instead.

Euphemisms serve as substitutes, and a foreigner needs to learn the code in order to understand what is really being said. For example, instead of saying that someone is sick, Arabs may describe a person as "a little tired." They avoid a word like *cancer*, saying instead "He has 'it'" or "She has 'the disease,'" and often wait until an illness is over before telling others about it, even relatives. Arabs do not speak easily about death and sometimes avoid telling others about a death for some time; even then they will phrase it euphemistically.

Some years back I was visiting the owner of an Egyptian country estate, when two men came in supporting a third man who had collapsed in the field. The landlord quickly telephoned the local health unit. He got through just as the man slipped from his chair and appeared to be having a heart attack. "Ambulance!" he screamed. "Send me an ambulance! I have a man here who's...a little tired!"

I also had an amusing experience listening to an American life insurance salesman discuss a policy with an Arab. "Now if you should be killed," he began, "or become paralyzed, or blind, or lose a limb...." The conversation ended rather quickly; the Arab decided he did not want to hear about that policy!

In technical situations, of course, where specificity is required (doctor to patient, commander to soldier), explicit language is used.

The Written Word

Arabs have considerable respect for the written as well as the spoken word. Some pious people feel that anything written in Arabic should be burned when no longer needed (such as newspapers) or at least not left on the street to be walked on or used to wrap things, because the name of God probably appears somewhere. Decorations using Arabic calligraphy, Qur'anic quotations, and the name "Allah" are never used on floors. They are often seen, however, in framed pictures or painted on walls. If you buy anything decorated with Arabic calligraphy, ask what it means; you could offend Arabs by the careless handling of an item decorated with a religious quotation.

If you own an Arabic Qur'an, you must handle it with respect. It should be placed flat on a table or in its own area on a shelf, not wedged in with many other books. Best of all, keep it in a velvet box or display it on an X-shaped wooden stand (both are made for this purpose). Under no circumstances should anything (an ashtray, another book) be placed on top of the Qur'an.

Written blessings and Qur'anic verses are effective in assuring safety and preventing the evil eye, so they are seen all over the Arab World. Blessings are painted on cars and trucks and engraved on jewelry. You will see religious phrases in combination with the color blue, drawings of eyes, or pictures of open palms, all of which appear on amulets against the evil eye.

Proverbs

Arabs make abundant use of proverbs, of which they have hundreds. Many are in the form of rhymes or couplets. A person's knowledge of proverbs and when to use them enhances his or her image by demonstrating wisdom and insight.

Here is a selection of proverbs that help illuminate the Arab outlook on life. Proverbs frequently refer to family and relatives, patience and defeatism, poverty and social inequality, fate and luck.

- Support your brother, whether he is the tyrant or the tyrannized.
- The knife of the family does not cut.
  (If you are harmed by a relative, don't take offense.)
- You are like a tree, giving your shade to the outside.
  (You should give more attention to your own family.)
- One hand alone does not clap.
  (Cooperation is essential.)
- The hand of God is with the group.
  (There is strength in unity.)
- The young goose is a good swimmer.
  (Like father, like son.)
- Older than you by a day, wiser than you by a year.
  (Respect older people and their advice.)
- The eye cannot rise above the eyebrow.
  (Be satisfied with your station in life.)
- The world is changeable, one day honey and the next day onions.
- Every sun has to set.
  (Fame and fortune may be fleeting.)
- Seven trades but no luck.
  (Even if a person is qualified in many trades, because of bad luck he may not find work.)
- It's all fate and chance.
- If a rich man ate a snake, they would say it was because of his wisdom; if a poor man ate it, they would say it was because of his stupidity.

- Your tongue is like a horse—if you take care of it, it takes care of you; if you treat it badly, it treats you badly.
- The dogs may bark but the caravan moves on.
  (A person should rise above petty criticism.)
- Patience is beautiful.
- A concealed sin is two-thirds forgiven.
- The slave does the thinking and the Lord carries it out.
  (Man proposes and God disposes.)
- Bounties are from God.
  (All good things come from God.)

And finally, my very favorite:

- The monkey in the eyes of his mother is a gazelle.
  (There's nothing quite like mother love!)

Conclusion

The more you socialize and interact with Arabs, the sooner you will abandon your stereotyped impressions of them. Individuals behave differently, but patterns emerge if you look for them. Soon you will be able to understand and even predict actions and reactions, some of which may be different from what you expected. Your task is to become aware of how and why things happen in order to feel comfortable with new social patterns as soon as possible.

Arab culture is complex but not unfathomable or totally exotic; many people find it similar to life in the Mediterranean area and Latin America.* Arabs are demonstrative, emotional, and full of zest for life, while at the same time bound by stringent rules and expectations. Westerners need not feel obliged to imitate Arabs in order to be accepted. All that is necessary for harmonious relations is to be nonjudgmental and to avoid any actions that are insulting or shocking. Westerners, especially Americans, are accustomed to being open and up-front with beliefs and feelings. This forthrightness needs to be tempered when operating in the tradition-bound culture of the Middle East.

---

* This is due, in part, to the fact that the Arabs ruled Spain for the seven centuries preceding the discovery of the New World.

Arabs are accustomed to dealing with foreigners and expect them to behave and dress differently and to have different ideas from themselves. Foreigners are forgiven a great deal; even conservative people make allowances, particularly when they trust your motives. The essential thing is to make a sincere, well-meaning effort to adapt and understand. This attitude is readily apparent and will go a long way in helping you form comfortable work relations and friendships. Perhaps you will find yourself on good enough terms with an Arab friend to ask for constructive criticism from time to time. If you do, tactful hints will be offered—listen for them.

Most Arabs are genuinely interested in foreigners and enjoy talking to and developing friendships with them. But their attitude toward Westerners is a mixture of awe, goodwill, and resentment. They admire Westerners' education and expertise, and most of them have heard favorable reports from others who have visited Western countries. Many Arabs express the hope that they can visit or study in the West, and in some countries, travel and immigration to Western countries are popular.

At the same time Arabs feel that Western societies are too liberal in many ways and that Westerners are not careful enough about their personal and social appearance. Arabs have a great deal of pride and are easily hurt; thus, they are sensitive to any display of arrogance by Westerners and to implied criticisms. They also disapprove of and resent Western political policies in the Arab World.

Moving to an Arab country or interacting with Arabs need not be a source of anxiety. If you use common sense, make an effort to be considerate, and apply your knowledge of Arab customs and traditions, it will be easy to conduct yourself in a way which reflects creditably on your background and home country and, at the same time, to have a rich and rewarding experience.

Appendix A

Muslims and Arabs in the West

There has been a sharp rise in both Arab and Muslim immigration to the West, which has affected their societies back home. The trend toward increased emigration (except from Saudi Arabia and the Gulf states) continues. Muslims and Arabs, however, are entirely different populations. Statistics for both of these groups are somewhat unreliable; estimates for both the United States and Europe vary widely.

Muslims in the United States and Canada

The Muslim population in the United States has increased 50 percent during the last ten years, and more than half of the Muslims live in California, New York, Michigan, Illinois, and New Jersey (Cohn 2001). By the year 2000, the number of mosques and Islamic centers had risen to 1,209 (up from about 900 ten years prior to that time), and participation in mosques increased 400 percent between 1994 and 2000 (Bagby and Bagby 2001).

Of the six to seven million Muslims in the United States, approximately 12 to 13 percent (750,000) are Arabs (Arabs constitute 20 percent of the total Muslim population worldwide) (Ruff 1998; Shaikh 1992). One-third of U.S. Muslims are African Americans, 80,000 are of Western European origin, and the others are of Mideastern origin. Ten thousand Muslims serve in the U.S. military (Blank 1998). There are about 500,000 Muslims in Canada (Haddad and Smith 2002, vi).

In the past twenty years, hundreds of Islamic schools have been opened, two-thirds of them at the primary level. Currently there are about 2,400 Islamic schools in the United States (Bagby and Bagby, 35, 36).

American immigrants of Middle Eastern ancestry are more affluent, better educated, and more likely to be married and have children than the average citizen. Among U.S. Muslims, 58 percent of the adults are college graduates (Culver 2002). In Canada the percentage of university graduates among Muslims is nearly three times that of the total Canadian population (Karim 2002, 264). In the United States, 77 percent of Muslims are active in organizations that help the poor, sick, elderly, and homeless. Sixty-nine percent are active in school and youth organizations, and 46 percent belong to a professional organization (Zogby 2001, 16). Ninety percent agree that Muslims should be involved in U.S. political institutions and should participate in the political process (Zogby, 17). Eighty-four percent favor tougher laws to prevent terrorism (Culver). In another poll, 79 percent of the Muslims were registered to vote and 96 percent favored participation in civic life (Lampman 2002).

In November 2000, 152 Muslims were elected to various local, city, and state offices (Saeed, 52). In Canada various Islamic programs and conferences have been funded by the federal multiculturalism program. (Karim, 269)

Islam is the second most commonly practiced religion in America, having surpassed Judaism in numbers (Blank, 22).

The vast majority of American Muslims were appalled by the terrorist attacks of 11 September 2001 and used every opportunity to emphasize that Al Qaeda's militant ideology and aberrant philosophy in no way represent mainstream Islamic thought. All of these people have a huge stake in the future welfare of Western countries.

Many Muslims believe that the mainstream majority has remained silent too long.* The theme of the December 2001 conference of the Muslim Public Affairs Council (MPAC) was "The Rising Voice of Moderate Muslims" (Lampman).† Terrorism has been defined and condemned by Muslim legal scholars; there is a distinction between terrorism and self-defense. Muslim and non-Muslim legal specialists are drawing up an "Islamic indictment" against Osama Bin Laden. Among other things, it will assert that Bin Laden exceeded his authority in issuing religious calls and judgments (Cooperman 2002a).

Arabs in the United States

There are more than three million people of Arab origin in the United States. Of these, 75 percent are Christian and 25 percent are Muslim (Arab American Institute 2000). Christians, especially Lebanese and Syrians, got a head start; they

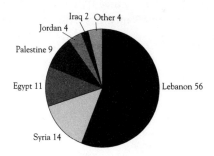

---

* This is discussed at length in Peter Ford (2001).
† See also the speech given by the executive director of MPAC on 28 January 2002, www.amila.org

began emigrating in the late nineteenth and early twentieth centuries. The Arabs who arrived during or after the 1960s are mostly Muslims.

The chart on the previous page shows Arab Americans' countries of origin by percentage.

Thirty-six percent of Arab Americans hold college degrees (compared with 20 percent of the U.S. population as a whole),‡ 72 percent work in professional and managerial jobs, and 82 percent are citizens (Samhan 1999).

In a poll conducted in late 2001, 69 percent of the Arab Americans supported an all-out war against countries that support and/or harbor terrorists (Arab American Institute 2001).

Muslims in Europe

Statistics for the number of Muslims in Europe are indefinite. Muslims come from numerous countries of origin, and Europe's secular governments tend to collect few religious statistics; furthermore, many Muslims are in Europe illegally (Bistofi 1995, 15, 17). In 2000 there were probably twenty to thirty million Muslims in Europe (including Eastern Europe) (Vertovec and Peach 1997, 13). Islam is the second most commonly practiced religion in Europe (*Britannica Book of the Year* 2001). Shown here are statistics that range widely and are all approximate (additional figures from some other sources are given in footnotes):

---

‡ Sixty percent of the Egyptians hold a bachelor's degree or above.

Number of Muslims in Western Europe in 2002[§]

Australia[‖]	200,000
Austria	400,000
Belgium	600,000
Denmark	150,000
France	5,500,000
Germany	3,200,000
Greece	600,000
Italy	1,000,000
Netherlands	900,000
Norway	60,000
Portugal and Spain	380,000
Sweden	400,000
Switzerland	400,000
United Kingdom	2,200,000

Shown below are the statistics for Muslims in Eastern Europe in 1996, the most recent data available (Nonneman, Niblock, and Szajkowski 1996, 40–49).

Number of Muslims in Eastern Europe 1996

Albania	1.7–2.2 million
Bulgaria	1.5 million
Czechoslovakia	2,000
Hungary	5,000
Poland[¶]	10,000–15,000[#]
Romania	60,000
Former Yugoslavia	5.5–7.5 million

[§] Federation of Islamic Organizations in Europe (2002). www.fioe.org The figure for Norway is from Naguib (2002), 161. The figure for Australia is from Saeed (2002), 195.

[‖] Australia is included here and on page 134 because it is a largely Western European society.

[¶] The number for Poland is from Vertovec and Peach (1997), 91.

Eastern European Muslims are mostly indigenous; their ancestors converted to Islam while the region was part of the Ottoman Empire. Estimates for the former USSR are very imprecise and are not included. One source quotes 55 to 75 million; another reports 11.4 million in Russia proper (Bistofi; Vertovec and Peach, 14).

Number of Mosques and Islamic Centers in Western Europe 2002**

Australia	80
Belgium	300
Denmark	60
France (1997)	1,200
Germany	1,200
Italy	180
Netherlands	400
Spain (1995)	41
United Kingdom	850

In France the number of Muslim "cultural sites" rose from ten to over one thousand between 1970 and 1985 (Pedersen 1999, 34).

Muslims in Western Europe originate from both Arab and non-Arab countries. For example, the Muslims in France are primarily from North and West Africa. Turks constitute the major (75 percent) Muslim population in Germany. In the United Kingdom the majority of Muslims are from South Asia. Turks and North Africans make up most of the primary

----

** The sources of data for these figures are as follows: Australia (Johns and Saeed 2002), Belgium (Friedman 2002b), Denmark (Simonsen 2002), France (Tlemcani 1997), Germany (Helicke 2002), Italy (Roggero 2002), Netherlands (Sunier and Kuijeren 2002), Spain (Shadid and van Konigsveld 1995), United Kingdom (Vertovec 2002).

groups in Switzerland, Scandinavia, Belgium, and the Netherlands. The mix in Spain is different still: North Africans and Pakistanis (Nielsen 1995).

Europe also receives waves of refugees periodically; it is affected far more than is the United States by destabilization in the Muslim world (Al-Janadriyya Festival 1995). Recently, for example, a large number of displaced persons from the Balkans entered Europe; they are not counted here.

There are some crucial differences in the population profiles of Muslims in Europe as compared with the United States. In the U.S., Mideastern immigrants are largely professional and middle class, whereas many in Europe are not well educated and constitute an underclass (many came in the 1960s when the demand for workers outstripped domestic resources). While most Muslims in the U.S. are viewed as citizens or potential citizens, in much of Europe they are still seen as immigrants. In Europe many Muslims are unmarried wage earners and do not intend to stay, whereas Muslim immigrants to the U.S. usually come with their families. Finally, Muslims in the U.S. are more geographically spread out than in Europe, where they are highly concentrated in certain cities and areas and many remain economically vulnerable and marginalized (Esposito 1995, 357–58).

Arabs in Western Europe

Number of Arabs in Western Europe 2002††

Austria	40,000
Belgium	320,000
Denmark	35,000
France	3,800,000
Germany	360,000
Greece	45,000

†† Federation of Islamic Organizations in Europe.

Italy	650,000
Netherlands	350,000
Portugal and Spain	260,000
Sweden	110,000
Switzerland	87,000
United Kingdom	500,000

Image in the West

Arabs (and Muslims) are often portrayed in Western media as excessively wealthy, irrational, sensuous, and violent, and there is little counterbalancing information about ordinary people who live family- and work-oriented lives on a modest scale. The media concentrate on reporting the sensational, not the truly typical. This misleading image has persisted for decades in North America and in Europe. No real distinction is made between Arabs and Muslims, and sometimes the religion of Islam is confused with Arab nationalism or with certain extremist segments of the Muslim community located outside of America.

Image in America

According to Dr. Yvonne Haddad, a specialist on Islam in America, Muslims have an image problem:

> For Muslims...discrimination has been aggravated as a consequence of growing hostility towards Islam in the West, sometimes called "Islamophobia." Recently, the religion factor has been especially significant. The stereotyping that has come from media responses to international events usually has repercussions on Muslims living in minority communities in the West. They become the focus of attention and of scapegoating. (Haddad and Smith, xii)

The problem of negative image led to the formation of the American-Arab Anti-Discrimination Committee (ADC) in

1980. Twenty-one years ago an observer remarked, "The Arabs remain one of the few ethnic groups who can still be slandered with impunity in America" (Slade 1981). Unfortunately, this image persists today. Recently, an Arab Muslim wrote,

> The decades-long Anti-Islam campaign waged by our [American] media, movies, and some "experts" has indoctrinated Americans to view anything Arabic or Islamic with prejudice and contempt.... [The] educational system must be revamped to include world history, religions, and cultures. (Khodr 2001)

Muslims as a whole are broadly stereotyped in the media.‡‡ This article in the *Christian Science Monitor* is illustrative.

> Today, despite multicultural awareness and education, stereotypes of Muslims persist in popular media. Islam is often equated with violence; Muslims are reduced to film clips of fist-shaking extremists. Yet the image misrepresents the majority of Muslims in the U.S.—who are successful, educated, and socially conservative. (Marquand 1996)

Such stereotypes have been well documented by the ADC and others (Shaheen 2001; Findley 2001; Shaheen 1997; Shaheen 1984). "In some cases the image of Muslims is tied to an irrational person, due to media focus—in countries such as Iran, Iraq, Sudan, Syria, Libya, Afghanistan, Palestine, and, occasionally, Pakistan" (Saeed, 44).

Mideasterners have stereotypes about the West too, mostly based on the lifestyle seen in Hollywood films or on television shows such as *Dallas*.

Since the attacks of 11 September 2001, Muslims have faced increased discrimination, threats, violence, and vandalism. From September 11 to December 6, 2001, the U.S. Equal Employment

---

‡‡ And in much popular literature. An example is given in Palumbo (1987), 212.

Opportunity Commission (EEOC) received more than double the complaints of discrimination toward Muslims in the workplace compared with the same period the previous year (166 vs. 64) (Grimsley 2001). There were 300 complaints by March of 2002, and a special category was created to track them (Sheridan 2002). In 2000 the FBI reported 33 anti-Islamic hate crimes across the country, whereas in the four months following September 11, authorities investigated more than 250 incidents (Cooperman 2002b).§§

Assaults, bomb threats, and vandalism of mosques and Muslim-owned property have long been a problem, and these increased markedly following September 11. An Islamic center in Columbus, Ohio, was vandalized, and since then, local residents have reached out to the Muslim community. They were offered space in a synagogue and in several churches as well as financial assistance from Jewish and Christian groups (Hoover 2002). Since September 11 between six and nine murders of Mideasterners were classified as hate crimes; victims included Indians and Sikhs who are not Muslim (Cooperman 2002b). In Canada mosques were damaged or destroyed in British Columbia and Manitoba (*Faith in Action* 2001). Hate crimes linked to the September 11 attack increased 90 percent in Canada in the following two months (Quinn 2002).

For some time Muslim women activists have protested hiring and employment problems related to their wearing the Hejab at work (Haddad and Esposito 1998, 110). In a highly publicized occurrence in November 2001, a Muslim woman was forced to remove her Hejab publicly in an airport, an event that has led to a lawsuit ("ACLU" 2002). A Muslim teenage girl who was forced to remove her Hejab in an airport in December 2001, later received an apology from the president of the airline ("Delta Apologizes" 2002). Muslims be-

§§ The nature and place of attacks are detailed at the Council on American-Islamic Relations Website, www.cair-net.org

lieve that Westerners have imposed their own interpretation on the Hejab; among non-Muslims, some insist that it symbolizes the repression of women.

Protests in Dallas in late 2001 led to an agreement between the *Dallas Morning News* and the Council on American Islamic Relations (CAIR), intended to revise the paper's manner of reporting about Muslims (*Faith in Action*).

All of this has happened before. During the first three days after the federal building in Oklahoma City was bombed in April 1995, 222 attacks were recorded against Muslims. Later, of course, it was determined that Muslims, inside and outside of the United States, had no role whatsoever in that tragedy ("Bias Against Muslims" 1995).

There is some room for optimism, though. At a conference in 1995, Dr. James Zogby, president of the Arab American Institute, stated,

> We have learned that while some widespread prejudices exist against Arabs and Muslims, they can be dispelled because they are largely the product of ignorance and a lack of information. (Al-Janadriyya Festival)[||||]

In many communities victims of attacks have received donations and hundreds of letters of support from their neighbors. In Mesa, Arizona, 1,200 people pledged to buy one month's groceries at a store where the owner, a Sikh, was killed (Cooperman 2002b). In cases of vandalism, Muslim worshippers have been offered accommodation in other houses of worship (Ghose 2002). After the 11 September 2001 attack, some mosques hosted open-house events and community outreach initiatives, which were well attended.

[||||] An excellent place to start remedying that lack is with the videos distributed by Films for the Humanities and Sciences; topics include "America from the Muslim Point of View," "The Islamic Wave," "Islamic Conversations," and "When the World Spoke Arabic."

Publicity after September 11 caused favorable views of Muslims to rise from 45 percent in March 2001, to 59 percent in December 2001 ("Post-September 11 Attitudes" 2001).

Image in Europe

A negative image of Arabs and Muslims is also extensively documented in Europe. At a 1988 conference titled "Information and Misinformation in Euro-Arab Relations," the following statement was made by Dr. Chedli Klibi, Secretary-General of the League of Arab States, in his opening address:

> In many areas of Western Europe the image of the Arab has greatly suffered, especially in recent decades, and mainly on account of media activity. Whether it be the stereotypes of the Gulf Arab, the disparaging way in which workers from the Maghreb are depicted, or the undiscriminating identification of Palestinian fighters as terrorists devoid of an ideal, the imagery of the Arabs in certain organs of the press, or even in certain widely read novels, inspires neither sympathy nor esteem. (20)

One writer described Muslims as "a brooding, menacing presence for many Europeans" (Ignatius 2002).

In Britain, negative views toward Muslims are widespread.

> Throughout the 1990s, this...has been fueled by national events like the Rushdie affair, and international developments, including terrorist activities by political Islamicists.... There has been a noticeable increase in derogatory images of Islam, patterns of anti-Muslim discrimination in employment, institutional intolerance of Muslim values, and occasional acts of physical violence against Muslims in Britain. (Vertovec, 24)

A particularly unfortunate event occurred following the Oklahoma City bombing. Much of world's press made immediate assumptions and blamed Islam. One of the worst blunders was committed by the British daily *Today*. Its front page on 20 April 1995 showed a picture of a fireman carrying a bloodstained baby under the banner headline, "In the Name of Islam" (Vertovec and Peach, 14).

In Germany, some say with bitterness, the government and society have always considered resident foreigners as "guest workers," even after many years. Most Germans "keep a suspicious distance" from Muslims. Both Arabs and Muslims as groups tend to withdraw to ghetto neighborhoods. Muslims find it difficult to practice Islam in Germany, and only about half of them actually do so (Abdullah 1995, 67, 76, 77).¶¶

Describing the situation in France, a scholar stated,

> The specificity of Islam in France lies in the fact that it is mainly viewed as a religion of the colonised, of poor people, of obscurantism, unable to adapt itself to French values (the term *integration* is very often used about people of Muslim culture) and in contradiction with French political rules. (Wenden 1996, 64)

In Denmark:

> Islam is seen as a patriarchal form of repression. The schools define Islam as constituting a pedagogical threat whose social consequences should be repressed.... Although there is a certain institutional tolerance, Islam is met with skepticism and distaste.... Islam is still considered to be a foreign religion. (Pedersen 1996, 209; 1999)

> An anti-immigrant political party doubled its votes in March, 2002. (Finn 2002)

In the Netherlands:

> A new image has made its way into the public discourse. This image is far from harmless and links Muslims in the Nether-

---

¶¶ The anti-immigrant National Front came in second in the first-round presidential election in April 2002 (Richberg 2002).

lands to the violence in the Middle East. Muslims are conceived as a fifth column that may be a threat to society. (Sunier and Kuijeren, 150)

In Italy:

Points of conflict do exist. The wave of racism and xenophobia which is spreading in Italy has targeted the Muslim element of society. Enmity toward Muslims, already perceptible during the Gulf War, is evident because of a growing fear of "Islamic fundamentalism." (Ianari 1995, 322–23)

In Spain:

Muslim groups, especially the recent immigrants, which are the most numerous and visible in the large cities, give to the presence of Muslims a look of marginalized proletarized classes, [and they are] an easy prey to suspicion and contempt, even violence and open xenophobia. This picture, together with the Islamic developments broadcast by the media, adds to the scornful and suspicious image the Spaniards create with regard to the Arab world and Islam. (Abumalham 1996, 84)

In Australia:

As a religious group, [Muslims] are perceived as a distinct group within Australian society, a perception associated with certain stereotypes and attitudes held by the majority community. The results of a recent survey [1989] conducted by the Office of Multicultural Affairs show that a majority of Australians regard Muslims negatively...Muslims face the highest level of prejudice. (Hassan 1995, 121)

In 1995 the situation was recognized by John Esposito, who has written much about Islam and the West.

The presence of significant Muslim minority populations puts strains on the social fabric of European societies like France, where Islam is the second largest religion, and Great Britain, where it is in third place. Anti-Arab/Muslim sentiment in

Western Europe is part of a growing xenophobia. Muslim communities and indigenous groups have clashed over questions of continued immigration, citizenship, and the accommodation of Muslim belief and practices. The tendency has been to exaggerate the magnitude and extent of the threat, as well as to place these questions in an "us" and "them" context. (Al-Janadriyya Festival)

Roger Ballard, a British scholar, summarized,

> What is striking is the intensity of the hostility which the very presence of a Muslim population [and] the articulation of the mildest of Islamic demands are currently precipitating in virtually every part of Europe where they have settled [this is] so much so that there is good reason to suggest that the visions of difference originally erected a thousand years ago are now being both revived and revised.... Islam has once again been represented as the antithesis of just those characteristics which Europe and the Europeans would like to believe that they themselves epitomise. (1996, 39–40)

Although Muslims around Europe complain about alienation and many feel like second-class citizens (Fisher 2001; Abedin and Sardar, 76–77), they are in fact becoming more active in civic affairs and political organizations; for example, there is one Muslim in the British Parliament. There are some 150 Muslim councilors [sic] in local government across Britain (Vertovec, 29). The number of Islamic organizations in Europe has doubled or even tripled in the last fifteen years (Ramadan 2002, 159).

There is no doubt that Muslims have long faced prejudice, toward themselves and toward their religion. The subject of Muslims in Europe has attracted a good deal of scholarship lately; much current commentary can be found in the proceedings of recent conferences.

Two topics have received much publicity in Europe: Islamic schools and headscarves.

Islamic Schools

Islamic schools in Europe are not nearly as numerous as they are in the United States. Some European countries, as is the case in the U.S., do not extend official recognition to religions. Some do extend it, some have an official state church, and others have an unofficial but strong religious tradition in their society. In a few countries the state subsidizes religious schools, which means that decisions must be made regarding Islamic schools as well.

There were about sixty Islamic schools in the United Kingdom in 2002 (Vertovec, 31). They were denied state subsidies for a time because the policy makers saw Islamic schools as a challenge to British authority. After a protest two schools were granted state support in 1998 and a third one in 2000 (Fazili 2001).

In the Netherlands and Denmark, which probably have the most favorable circumstances for establishing Islamic schools, political debate continues. About thirty Islamic schools in the Netherlands are subsidized (Sunier and Kuijeren, 144), as are fourteen in Denmark (Pedersen 1996, 208). In Belgium the establishment of Islamic schools was blocked; the only exception is one primary school in Brussels, which is government-subsidized (Nielsen). In Berlin one school is subsidized (Stowasser 2002, 66), and there are no Islamic schools in Norway (Vogt 2002, 98).

Headscarves

The wearing of headscarves is an interesting issue that represents Muslims' attempt to maintain their own cultural and religious traditions while living in the West.

Muslim girls' right to wear headscarves in state schools became controversial in Europe in the 1980s. In France the right of female Muslim students to wear headscarves in the Hejab style was challenged officially in 1989 and then banned.

(This is in keeping with the tradition of French state schools that forbid outward symbols of religion.) After the discussion escalated from the local to the national level, the government stated that girls may wear headscarves, providing this is not done as an "act of proselytism" but merely as an expression of religious background. The situation in Belgium was similar: the prohibition against headscarves was revoked in 1989, and there are no central rules; the issue is determined by local authorities. In the Netherlands this issue still causes conflicts; prohibition was revoked in 1985, although private Christian schools retain the right to regulate headscarves (Shadid and van Konigsveld 1996, 95). Muslim women there have encountered problems with headscarves, however, in schools and offices (Sunier and Kuijeren, 154).

When the issue arose in Britain, there were various local compromises (Shadid and Konigsveld, 95). Scarves are permitted, but they must be tied tightly during physical education classes, and some schools require that their color match school uniforms.

The issue of headscarves has not died out in Europe. In France the ruling is still unclear; France's Human Rights Report of 1999 stated that "no national decision has been reached," and the State Council of France once again reaffirmed the ban on headscarves in public schools. In Germany and also in Switzerland (Mahnig 2002, 77), students may wear headscarves in state schools, but teachers cannot. An applicant for a teaching job in Germany was denied a position because her scarf was declared "a political symbol of female submission rather than a religious practice prescribed in Islam" and designated "unacceptable for a teacher as a role model."***

***The teacher sued and the court upheld the action of the school, on the grounds that teachers have a legal responsibility of "neutrality" which overrides considerations of religious freedom (Fazili).

Women wearing headscarves may teach in German state schools only when studying for teaching degrees, but they are not allowed to take a permanent teaching position.

A Geneva, Switzerland, decison has been appealed to the European Court of Human Rights (Mahnig, 77). In Denmark the media reported in 1999 that most Danes viewed the Hejab as a sign of male dominance and female suppression (Simonsen, 127). There have been no reported problems in Italy (Roggero, 141).

* * * * * * *

In conclusion, Arabs, Muslims (and other Mideasterners) are now so numerous in both America and Europe that they are beginning to have noticeable effects on those societies, and their numbers will likely continue to increase. Conferences and public education campaigns will be crucial. The 11 September 2001 attacks in the United States created bewilderment and heightened curiosity about the Middle East, its people, its social and cultural practices, its religious traditions, and its political problems. Now is the time for more constructive engagements with Arabs and Muslims.

Appendix B

The Arab Countries: Similarities and Differences

Generalizing about Arabs is a little like generalizing about Europeans—they have many traits in common, but regional differences are striking. Arabs are more alike than Europeans, however, because they share the same language and, most importantly, they believe strongly that they are a cultural unit, one Arab nation. Arab nationalism has a broad appeal, despite shifting political alliances.

The national, social, and cultural characteristics briefly described below reveal some notable differences among various Arab national groups. The most important single difference that affects foreigners is the distinction between the conservatism of Saudi Arabia (and to some extent, the rest of the Arabian Peninsula) and the more liberal, or tolerant, ways of life elsewhere.*

---

* Unless otherwise identified, statistics in this section are taken from the *Middle East Review* 2000, *The Middle East and North Africa 2001* (2001), or the *World Factbook, 2001* (2001).

It is important to realize the differences among these countries; some are rich, others are poor. Relative prosperity can be seen from per capita income in 1998 (adjusted for purchasing power parity), and an updated estimated income in 2000/2001.

	Per capita income 1998($US)	Estimated 2000/2001($US)
Algeria	$ 4,380	$ 5,500
Bahrain	13,700	15,900
Egypt	3,130	3,600
Iraq	(n.a.)	2,500
Jordan	3,230	3,500
Kuwait	22,300	15,000
Lebanon	6,150	5,000
Libya	(n.a.)	8,900
Morocco	3,120	3,500
Oman	8,690	7,700
Qatar	17,690	20,300
Saudi Arabia	9,480	10,500
Sudan	1,330	1,000
Syria	3,000	3,100
Tunisia	5,160	6,500
UAE	19,720	22,800
Yemen	740	820

The Arab countries discussed below are listed from west to east, north to south.

Morocco

Morocco, a monarchy, has been strongly influenced by its proximity to Europe and its colonization by France until independence in 1956. Educated Moroccans are bilingual in Arabic and French, and although a campaign of Moroccanization has been under way, French is still needed for most professional and social advancement. Spanish is widely spoken in northern Morocco, and a growing minority of Moroccans, particularly younger people with commercial interests, now speak English.

Although a few Moroccans are of Arabian origin, most are descended from native Berber stock. Thirty-three to 40 percent of the population are Berbers, who are distinct from the Arab-Berber majority in that they speak Berber as their native language and identify themselves as Berbers first. Berber nationalism is growing; for example, the language is now heard on the radio. Berbers mainly inhabit the interior highlands of the Atlas Mountains. There are also many Moroccans of sub-Saharan African descent, especially in the southern part of the country.

The royal family traces its descent from the Prophet Muhammad. King Hassan II ruled for 38 years before his death in July, 1999; his son King Muhammad VI now rules, and he is making efforts toward political liberalization.

There are three distinct social classes: the royal family and a small educated elite, a growing middle class composed of merchants and professionals, and a lower class that includes more than half of the people. The population is about 30 million, with a growth rate that is among the highest in the world. Thirty-eight percent of the Moroccans are under the age of fifteen, and conditions are even worse in the north, where this number is over 50 percent (Edwards 1996). Fully 70 percent of the population is under the age of 25.

Tribalism is important in Morocco, particularly in the rural areas. Traditional farming remains the occupation of about half of the population. Since the trend toward urbanization, which began early in the twentieth century, cities have grown rapidly (the largest is Casablanca with a population of 3.5 million) (Edwards), resulting in expanding slums with many poor and underemployed urban residents. Fifty-eight percent of the population now lives in urban areas.

The unemployment rate was 23 percent in 1999 (it is higher in the north). Because of this, about 1.7 million Moroccan men work outside the country, mainly in France and Spain. Serious housing shortages continue in urban areas, and health care is still inadequate, with a rate of 0.5 physicians per 1,000 people.

Education has increased greatly since Morocco's independence—literacy rose from 15 percent in 1978 to 45 percent in 1999. Both French and Arabic are taught in schools. Eighty-six percent of age-eligible children are in primary school, and 39 percent are in secondary school.

Educated women in Morocco have been entering the professions for a generation, especially in the urban areas. Half of the students in universities are women; 20 percent of the judges in Morocco are women (Fernea 2000, 30). Although older and more conservative Moroccan women continue to veil in public, most women do not, nor do they always wear the traditional long cloak. Child custody laws were improved for women in 1994. Controversy regarding the amendment of women's legal rights is still strong. In March 2000, 400,000 people took to the streets in response to a proposal on the subject—half were for it, half were against it (Sachs 2001).

Although about 99 percent of the Moroccans are Muslims, other religions have always been practiced freely. Half of the Jews in the Arab World are in Morocco, some 10,000 (from a high of 350,000 in the 1950s) (Lamb 1995). Morocco's 70,000 Christian residents are of European origin. The practice of Islam is often mixed with local folk practices, such as the veneration of saints' tombs and their artifacts. Religious brotherhoods, mainly Sufis, are also common.

The Moroccan economy is largely dependent on agriculture, tourism, and phosphate mining (Morocco is the world's largest exporter of phosphates). About 40 percent of the workforce is employed in agriculture and fishing. The textile industry has become increasingly important; the number of textile workers has doubled, probably tripled, since the mid-1980s ("Historical Ties" 1993).

Moroccans are friendly and hospitable and usually very interested in becoming acquainted with foreigners. The elite are at ease with Westerners because of their exposure to French and European cultures.

Algeria

Algeria is a revolutionary socialist state where Arabization is strongly emphasized, partly as a reaction to the Algerians' experience with French colonization and their long, traumatic war. Independence was achieved in 1962, at a terrible cost—one million Algerians and 28,000 French dead ("Historical Ties"). Despite the fact that Arabic is the official language of the country, French is still widely spoken, particularly for professional purposes. Both languages are taught in the schools, but only younger Algerians are truly comfortable with Standard (written) Arabic.

Arab nationalism is strong, promoted through government political campaigns, the news media, and the school curriculum. Algeria is in the midst of a desperate political and humanitarian crisis. Open warfare exists between the government and ever-growing numbers of fundamentalist Islamic activists, the most prominent of which is the Islamic Salvation Front (FIS), which was formally recognized by the government in 1989. In 1990 FIS candidates gained control in municipal and gubernatorial elections (54 percent of the popular vote), and in January 1992, fearing their total victory, the government called off national elections and banned the organization. Since then, there has been a rising cycle of violent attacks, many of them random, many in villages. Violence is an everyday occurrence; in some weeks 300 to 400 people are killed. These killings are met with severe government retaliation. By 2001 about 80,000 people had been killed, possibly as many as 100,000, and the population is now polarized between secular and Islamic groups, radicals and moderates (Kaplan 1998, 20; Lerch 2001; Lancaster 1998). Almost all foreigners have left the country.

Most Algerians are of Berber ethnic origin, but about 69 percent identify themselves as Arabs and 30 percent as Berbers. Arabic is the native language of 80 percent of the people; the others speak Berber or are bilingual. Algeria's social classes consist of a small professional and technocratic elite, a growing middle class, and a large number of poor people. The long war for independence resulted in the massive displacement of people from their ancestral land and social groups, the psychological consequences of which will be felt for a very long time.

Two-thirds of Algeria is in the Sahara Desert; yet the temperate northern coastal region consists of excellent agricultural land and supports the employment of about one-fourth of the people. Algeria's population is 30 million, and its rate of growth is one of the highest in the world (75 percent are under age 30)—schools operate in shifts, the housing situation is desperate, and health-care facilities and providers cannot keep up; some poorer families even sleep in shifts. The population is expected to reach 52 million by 2025, a fivefold increase since 1950 ("Where the North" 1993). By 1998, 820,000 Algerians were working outside the country, mainly in France, because local salaries were low and prices were high at home. Unemployment is over 30 percent. Still, people continue to move from the sparsely populated south to the crowded northern cities seeking work.

Algeria is the world's largest producer of liquefied natural gas and has additional income from oil, mining, and agriculture. Because of the rapid population growth, however, prosperity remains elusive. Despite the government's efforts to diversify (95 percent of foreign earnings are from oil and gas) and industrialize the economy, Algeria, which produced 73 percent of its own food in 1969, was importing 75 percent of its food by 1990. The government has stated that it will try to reduce this dependence by 10 percent by 2004 (*The Middle East and North Africa 2001*, 335).

When Algeria gained its independence in 1962, there were few well-trained Algerians, and it has taken two generations to recover from the loss of the French managerial class. Now, however, a fast-growing number of educated Algerians are entering professional and technical fields. Almost half of Algeria's university graduates are women (Kaplan, 28), and they make up 24 percent of the workforce.

Family and social traditions are conservative, and more women veil in Algeria than in any other North African country. Algerian women had participated actively during the struggle for independence, so many felt betrayed when, in 1984, the government instituted the Family Code, which still restricts women's rights of divorce and custody and legalizes polygamy.

Algerians are accommodating but reserved. Although militant Islam has turned some people's sentiment against the West, many younger people are ready to befriend Westerners when they visit the country.

Tunisia

Tunisia is a small but diverse country that gained its independence from France in 1956. Since then it has been governed by one secular political party. President Habib Bourguiba, who led the country to independence, was quietly removed in 1987; his successor is President Zayn Al-Abdin Ben Ali. Because Tunisians have always had considerable contact with foreigners, their society is cosmopolitan, at least in the cities, and many Tunisians are well traveled. They are friendly and hospitable to foreign visitors.

The Tunisians are descended from Berber and Arab stock, but all speak Arabic, the official language. Educated people are bilingual in Arabic and French, and many semieducated people speak some French. French is taught in the schools alongside Arabic, but there is currently a campaign for the Arabization of education.

Because the Tunisian government encourages private enterprise, about 60 percent of the people are upper and middle class. Tunisia is considered by many as the most egalitarian country in the Arab World. The U.S. State Department has called it "a trendsetter in successful economic reform, a standard which other countries seek to duplicate" (Borowiec 1996).

The Tunisian economy depends mainly on a large tourism industry as well as on exported agricultural products and on the production of some oil and natural gas. The government is encouraging diversification and light industry, the latter of which is quickly becoming an important source of employment; in 1998 light industry generated about 22 percent of the national income. Three-fourths of Tunisia's exports go to Europe ("Europe Slow to Invest" 1993). Of the relatively small population of 9 million, about a third work in agriculture. Although the government has established agricultural cooperatives and production has been rising, people are still moving to the cities, where they join the urban poor, living in crowded conditions.

The Tunisian government spends a large proportion of its money on education; 95 percent of primary school-aged children are in school, and the literacy rate is 90 percent for people under age 35. This has unfortunately resulted in a large number of unemployed, educated young people; the unemployment rate is 16 percent. At the same time there is a shortage of skilled workers. Tens of thousands of Tunisian men work outside the country, mainly in France and Libya. The biggest problem in Tunisia is political; the government is threatened by growing Islamic fundamentalist activism. Due to harsh means used to suppress the fundamentalists, it has come under criticism from human rights organizations.

Tunisia has been at the forefront of the Arab nations in its efforts to liberalize its society. Tunisian women are certainly the most liberated in the Arab World; they are well educated and active in the workplace in such fields as education, social services, health care, office administration, and the judicial system. Laws benefiting women were enacted in the 1950s; then-President Bourguiba styled himself as "the Liberator of Women." Women have the same divorce rights as men. While most women wear Western clothing, older or traditional women wear loose outer cloaks, which they pull over to partially cover their faces when they are in public. The government has banned the wearing of headscarves in government offices and in schools (Borowiec).

Ninety-eight percent of Tunisians are Muslim. Only about 300 native Jews remain, and there are some Christians of European origin. Islam in Tunisia is mixed with a number of folk practices, such as veneration of saints' tombs. Its central city of Kairouan is a site of pilgrimages, because of its antiquity and importance to Islam.

Libya

Libya is the only North African nation that was colonized by Italy. Full rule was restored to the Libyan monarchy in 1949. Since the monarchy was overthrown in 1969, Libya has been governed by a leftist military regime under Colonel Muammar Qaddhafi, who has introduced radical socialist and economic development programs, instituted a strong campaign to educate and politicize the people, and set up programs to spur rapid social change. Because of his support for radical revolutionary movements, Libya has become something of a pariah state.

Until recently, most Libyans outside the cities were farmers or tribal seminomads, who were largely uneducated and lived simply. In 1951 Libya was considered one of the poorest countries in the world (*The Middle East and North Africa 2001*, 881). When oil was discovered in 1959, its effect on the economy was immediate. By 1969 the country's revenues were twenty times greater than they had been in 1962 (Allen 1981, 22). The economy is strained due to U.S. sanctions, which have been in effect since 1986, and to U.N. sanctions from 1992 to April of 1999. National income declined 7 percent from 1993 to 1994. Although the economy is now improving, unemployment is 30 percent.

Libya is a welfare state, and a considerable share of its oil income makes its way to the lower classes, who have experienced a dramatic rise in their standard of living, although there are still shortages of some basic goods and foodstuffs. There are steady improvements in health and nutrition programs, transportation, and communications. Before oil came, 25 percent of the population were urbanized; the figure is now 70 percent.

Libyans are a homogeneous ethnic group of mixed Berber and Arab descent, and all speak Arabic. Tribalism is an important source of identity, particularly among rural people. Although there are no officially recognized social classes now because of the government's policy of strict egalitarianism and rule "by the people," in reality rule is authoritarian, and only a few people are part of the elite upper class.

Libya's economic viability is almost entirely dependent on oil; its soil is poor, its natural resources and water sparse. Less than 10 percent of the land is suitable for agriculture (90 percent is desert), and 75 percent of the country's food is imported. Because Libya badly needs trained and skilled workers, large numbers of foreigners have lived and worked there, approximately 1 to 1.5 million in 1995, before Qaddhafi expelled large numbers of them, mainly Egyptians, Sudanese, and Palestinians. Libya's population is small, about 5.5 million, and, like elsewhere, there is continual migration from the rural areas to the cities.

Universal education has been available since the 1970s, and now 67 percent of the people are literate. Libya has supported tens of thousands of students in their study abroad, many of them in the United States. Libyan women now constitute 21 percent of the workforce, and they are encouraged to work in education, nursing, clerical services, and factory jobs.

Libyans are conservative and 99 percent Muslim, and Islamic law is generally followed, although with some modifications. The government promotes Islam, although this is mixed with a strong revolutionary message in order to guide social change and control dissent (some of the Islamic innovations and modifications have been denounced by religious authorities elsewhere). Arab nationalism and pan-Arab unity are extolled. Libyans are not encouraged to interact with foreigners and are hesitant to display customary Arab hospitality toward Westerners. As a result the people have relatively little contact with foreigners.

Egypt

Egypt's long history and ancient traditions have resulted in a homogeneous and distinctive society with a unique culture. Egyptians all speak Arabic, except for some Nubians in the far south, and English is the most common second language. French is also spoken by many.

Egypt has by far the largest population of any Arab nation, approximately 70 million in 2001. The population doubled between 1947 and the early 1980s; its rate of increase was as high as 4.1 percent per year in the late 1980s. But as a result of vigorous government campaigning, the rate decreased to 1.7 percent in 2001. Because only 4 percent of Egypt's land is habitable (the rest is desert), its population density is among the highest in the world. In 1995 there were over a thousand people per square kilometer of arable land (*Regional Surveys: The Middle East and North Africa* 1995).

About 10 percent of the Egyptians are in the elite upper class, which dominates the country socially and politically. The middle class is expanding; nevertheless, about 55 percent of the people are still peasant farmers or villagers, and there are many urban poor.

Because of its long tradition of education for the upper and middle classes, Egypt has an abundance of professionally trained citizens. In 1996 there were about 2.2 million Egyptians working abroad as teachers, doctors, accountants, and laborers. Until the mid-1980s the largest percentage of expatriate Egyptians were in the Arabian Peninsula and Libya. Since then most have been forced to leave because of the decline of the oil industry in the host nations. Unemployment is 15 to 20 percent overall, and in the younger age group, it runs to 70 percent, creating a serious social problem,

Intensive agriculture has always been central to the Egyptian economy. The government promotes industry and manufacturing; the main sources of income are oil, cotton, and other agricultural products. Tourism is the most important of all. Egypt's relative poverty makes it heavily dependent on aid from the United States. Once an exporter of food (since ancient times), Egypt now produces only 22 percent of the food needed for local consumption.

The Egyptian government has been socialist since 1952, when the current regime took power. Although it is stable, it faces a serious challenge from several militant Islamic movements, the most prominent of which are the Muslim Brotherhood and the Islamic Group. These groups are illegal, however, and members are subject to arrest (Waxman 2001). Islamist organizations have gained support because they provide social services not available from the government; this has been especially noticeable in times of disasters. There have been several terrorist attacks, mainly against the government but even against tourists. The government has reacted harshly and continues to make widespread arrests, bring Islamists to trial, and hold thousands (29,000 in 1994) in custody. As goodwill gestures, the government released 5,000 Islamists in 1998 and 5,000 in 1999 (Schneider 2001). Discussion of this issue is a constant feature in the Egyptian press. Almost all of the 60,000 mosques are now regulated by the state.

Egyptians are hardworking but poor. Labor unrest and strikes in early 1999 were at the highest level since the revolution in 1952 (*The Middle East and North Africa 2001*, 444). Health has improved dramatically due to government programs instituted in the 1960s; unfortunately, education has not fared as well. Despite the fact that free education has been available to all children since the 1960s, the rate of literacy is still only about 51 percent (63 percent for men, 40 percent for women).

Egyptian women have enjoyed considerable personal freedom in pursuing their interests and have been integrated into the workforce at all levels for many years. Half the university students are women (Fernea, 29). Egypt was in fact the first Arab country to admit women to its national university, in 1928, and education is entirely coed. In 1957 two Egyptian women were the first to serve in an Arab parliament (Tucker 1991, 4), and there are more than 300 women's organizations in Cairo (Fernea). Although most Egyptian women have not covered their faces in the past, a growing number of women (more than half) in the past twenty years have made the decision to wear the Hejab. Many wear very conservative dress.

About 90 percent of the Egyptians are Muslims; about 10 percent are (officially) Christians, mostly Copts (the Coptic church estimates 15 percent) (Daniszewski 1997b). Islam is Egypt's official religion, but religious tolerance has long been practiced. There have been serious clashes with Islamic extremists, however, especially in the early 1990s, which worries the Christians. Egyptian society, which was among the most liberal in the Arab World in the 1960s and 1970s, has become more conservative.

Egypt is vibrant with cultural energy; it is the leader of the Arab nations in such fields as filmmaking and journalism. It has long been a dominant political and cultural influence in the Arab World, partly because of its large population, which makes up about 40 percent of all the Arabs. The Egyptian people are known to be friendly and good-humored, and they are very outgoing toward foreigners.

Sudan

Sudan is the largest country in Africa, with an area of one million square miles. It is tribal and diverse, with considerable sub-Saharan African influence on its social structure and ethnic composition. Tribalism is dominant throughout the society, and many men are marked with identifying facial scars, as is common in sub-Saharan Africa.

Arabic is spoken by only 60 percent of the population, although an Arabization program has been in place for decades. There are more than 600 ethnic groups in Sudan, speaking more than 400 languages (Finnegan 1999, 50). In many areas the early years of school are taught in the local language. Many people are bilingual in Arabic and their regional language, but Arabic is the only official language and is needed for social advancement.

Northern Sudanese are Arabs (in culture, not in ethnicity), and about 70 percent of the Sudanese people are Sunni Muslim; about 5 percent are Christian, mainly in the south, and the rest adhere to local or indigenous religions. Some tribes still live autonomously, barely influenced by the government, and some areas still do not have a cash economy. The Sudanese government decreed Islamic law in 1983, and since 1989 Sudan has had the only Islamist (fundamentalist) government in place in the Arab World (although not in the Middle East). The government is attempting to modernize within the Islamic system.

There has been an ongoing civil war between the Arab Islamic north and the African south virtually since Sudan's independence from the United Kingdom in 1956. The conflict has escalated since 1983, and a rebel army in the south continues its resistance. The war has been devastating—this is one of the world's worst sustained conflicts since World War II. Large-scale famine and unchecked disease continue to ravage the south; about two million are dead and four to five million have been displaced from their homes, mostly civilians in the south (the largest number of displaced persons in the world) (Greenberg and Shestack 2000; Finnegan, 71). The government has repeatedly been accused of genocide, human rights abuses, and the toleration of slavery; the world views the situation as a major humanitarian crisis. Thousands of people, including orphaned or abandoned children, are living in refugee camps. Many international relief organizations are present, both in the south and among the people in camps around Khartoum. In January 2002 the United States announced that it will mediate peace talks between the Sudanese government and the rebels (Osman 2002).

In 1993 Sudan was placed on the U.S. list of countries that sponsor international terrorism. The United States imposed comprehensive economic sanctions in 1997, and these were extended in November 2001 (Vick 2001). The U.S. is also funding the opposition alliance ("Pressure on Sudan" 2001).

The American embassy was closed in 1996, and in 1998 the United States carried out a cruise missile attack, which (notoriously) destroyed a pharmaceutical plant. Osama Bin Laden came to Sudan after he was expelled from Saudi Arabia, and it was there that he set up the Al Qaeda organization (Vick).

Sudan's economy has been one of the poorest and least developed in the world, but since 1998 oil has flowed, providing the government with ample funds for sustaining its war. The southern region has huge economic potential in its oil and minerals, rare timbers, and abundant water (Daniszewski 1997a).

Population density is low in Sudan, with a population of about 36 million in the entire country. Five million live in Khartoum. The government has promoted irrigation and land reclamation projects to develop the immense agricultural potential of much of the country (Sudan could feed almost all of Africa if it were developed). About 65 percent of the people are villagers and small farmers or herders. Tourism could be a potential draw, although by now, much of the big game that flourished a generation ago is gone.

Education has been available for the upper and middle classes for decades, and literacy for this group is 90 percent for men and 60 percent for women (in the north). Although there is a large pool of well-educated Sudanese professionals, because of low salaries at home, many work abroad, mainly in the Arabian Peninsula. This has caused a shortage of trained manpower in the country; at the same time, the overall unemployment rate is 20 percent.

Although education of women is increasing, only about 26 percent of Sudanese women work outside the home, mainly as teachers and social workers. Sudan is extremely conservative in its view of women's rights. Women do not cover their faces, but they all wear a long cloak and voluminous scarves in public.

Sudanese are known throughout the Arab world as friendly, sincere, generous, and scrupulously honest, and they are proud of this reputation. At the same time, they are religious and conservative.

Lebanon

Lebanon is a small country, both in size and in population (about four million), with a diverse geography and a long history of commercial and maritime importance. Its people are mainly descended from the same Semitic stock, but religious diversity and social class have been divisive and have created barriers to social integration. All Lebanese feel an intense loyalty to their own clan or religious group.

From 1975 to 1991, Lebanon experienced a disastrous civil war, during which 25 percent of the population was displaced and at least 130,000 people were killed. Religious tensions were in part the cause—the Christians (30 percent) have traditionally had more wealth and power than have the more numerous Muslims (70 percent), who in turn are divided among Sunnis and Shiites. The majority of the Christian Lebanese are of the native Maronite rite, and eleven other Christian denominations are recognized. Of the Muslims, about 26 percent are Sunni (or orthodox) and 27 percent are Shiite. A third influential denomination is the Druze religion, which originated in Lebanon in the eleventh century and is derived from Shiite Islam. Altogether, five Muslim sects are officially recognized. The social and political effects of this mix of religions and sects can well be imagined.

The Lebanese speak Arabic, and educated people also speak French, English, or both. Some minority groups, notably the Armenians, speak their own languages.

Prior to the beginning of the civil war, the Lebanese government was pro-Western and procapitalist, and the country was a leader in service industries such as banking and commerce and in the development of tourism. The Lebanese had the highest standard of living in the Arab World and the most cosmopolitan, sophisticated way of life, at least in Beirut. After Cairo, Beirut was the second largest center for the diffusion of Arab culture.

Since the end of the war, Lebanon has rebuilt extensively and recovered its infrastructure. It is gradually reclaiming many of the services for which it was known, and many of the people who fled to Europe or the United States during the war have returned. Prosperity is evident everywhere. But there are still between 400,000 and 600,000 Palestinian refugees in Lebanon (Collelo 1989, 53).

There are clearly defined social classes in Lebanon, with a small upper class, a growing middle class, and a large lower class made up of about half of the people. The lower classes are quite poor, and the majority live in urban areas. Agricultural production is limited by inadequate natural resources, and imports far exceed exports. Unemployment is about 18 percent.

Lebanese have migrated abroad in great numbers since the late nineteenth century (more live outside the country than inside), and sustained contacts with these emigrants all over the world has influenced the society and economy. Many Lebanese work in other Arab countries, mainly as managers and professionals, and they are known for their commercial ability and resourcefulness.

The Lebanese are highly educated. Free public education has long been available, and the literacy rate in urban areas is 86 percent, one of the highest in the Arab World. In the mid-nineteenth century, French and American missionaries established schools in Lebanon that trained many future leaders and intellectuals of the Arab World and brought Western influence strongly to bear on their culture. Standards of health care and social services are once again high, as they were before the war.

Urban Lebanese women, especially Christians, are active in the professions, commerce, and social organizations. They generally dress in the Western manner and mix freely in society. In contrast women in rural areas are restricted by the prevailing traditional values.

The Lebanese people are well traveled and sophisticated, and they are politically oriented and concerned about their position in the world. Some, mainly Christians, believe that Lebanon should be more Western than Arab and should identify with Europe; others, mainly Muslims, identify with pan-Arab sentiments and want to de-emphasize Western influences. The society remains divided.

Syria

Syrian civilization has reached high levels in its long history, but it has also been subjected to frequent invasions and conquests, mainly because of its strategic location. The nation's population is diverse. Of its 17 million people, about

85 percent are Muslims (70 percent of those are Sunni, the rest belong to other Islamic sects). Minority groups in Syria include Christians, 5 to 10 percent, and Druze, 3 percent. Of the Sunni Muslims, one-tenth are Kurds. The most notable Muslim sect is that of the Alawites, who have controlled the government since 1970, when the current regime took power. Jews are no longer a significant part of the population; only 400 or so remain, and they mostly live in Damascus (Lamb 1995).

Syria's socialist government is authoritarian, strongly nationalistic, and cautious in its relations with the West. With the death of President Hafez Al-Assad in 2000, Bashar, his son, assumed the presidency, and he appears to be making efforts to liberalize the country and to reform the economy; nevertheless, the future remains hard to predict (MacFarquhar 2001). Syria has been accused of supporting international terrorism, which affects both its tourism and its trade. It has off-and-on relations with other Arab countries; the Syrian army has long been a strong presence (25,000 troops at this time) in Lebanon. Fundamentalism is not a threat; President Assad put down an Islamist rebellion in Hama in 1982 in which at least 10,000 civilians died.

Syria is one of the more densely populated Arab countries. About half of its land is habitable, and the population growth rate is such that 44 percent of the people are under age 14. The upper and middle classes make up about 35 percent of the population. Education and health care are widely available, and literacy has reached 90 percent for men, 60 percent for women. Agricultural production is an important factor in the economy, as are oil, phosphates, and textiles. Land reform and the establishment of agricultural cooperatives have led to improvements in the lives of small farmers, who make up about one third of the population. The standard of living in urban areas has also improved. New government policies are designed to attract foreign investment and rejuvenate the economy. Unemployment is about 20 percent.

Most Syrians identify strongly with Arab nationalism and their Arab/Muslim heritage; they are generally quite conservative. Few Western tourists have visited Syria in recent decades, so contact is fairly recent and tourism is just getting started. French is more widely spoken than English.

Syrian women of the upper class have been well educated for two generations and are moderately active in the workforce, especially as teachers and social and health-care workers. Most of them dress in the Western manner. Twenty-six of the 250 members of Parliament are women (Beyer 2001, 59).

Syrians are friendly and very hospitable. They are interested in world events and enjoy discussions about a wide range of subjects. Syria is starting to open up.

Jordan

Jordan is a relatively new nation. It was created under the British mandate at the end of World War I and achieved its independence in 1946. Jordan's former West Bank (of the Jordan River, occupied by Israel since 1967) was formally ceded to the Palestinians in 1988. The East Bank (now Jordan proper) was originally tied by Hashemite tribal affiliations with northwest Saudi Arabia (the Hejaz).

About 60 percent of Jordan's 5 million people are of Palestinian origin, most of whom arrived after the events of 1948 and 1967. Most are well educated and many are wealthy. Palestinians are regarded as loyal and productive; they all hold Jordanian citizenship and have the same political and economic rights as Jordanians. There are still, however, 220,000 Palestinians in refugee camps (Viorst 1991, 35). About 5 percent of Jordan's citizens are of Bedouin origin, although tribalism is rapidly giving way as more people settle in or near cities, a development encouraged by the government.

Jordan's monarchist government is Hashemite (descended from the Prophet), and during King Hussein's reign of 47 years, it was, for the most part, moderate and pro-Western. After the king's death in February 1999, his son Abdullah assumed the throne and has been promoting further efforts toward economic and political openness. There is some opposition from the fundamentalist Muslim Brotherhood, which won a majority of seats in parliamentary elections in 1989. Jordan is probably the most democratic of all Arab countries; the king's goal is to serve as a model for the entire region. Parliamentary elections are scheduled for summer 2002.

Jordan is, however, poor in resources, and despite numerous economic initiatives, the nation is still largely dependent on foreign aid. Only 6 percent of the land is arable, and 20 percent of the people are farmers. A notably successful innovation has been a microfund program that lends small amounts of money to low-income women. Established in 1996, it has already made over 61,000 loans (Harrington 2001).

Jordan's location between Israel and Iraq is a disadvantage; it has suffered because of both neighbors. Before the Gulf War, 75 percent of its trade was with Iraq ($1 billion per year); this was reduced to one quarter of that amount (MacFarquhar). Jordan depends on Iraq for oil, and many Jordanians feel a cultural kinship with Iraqis. Jordan's crucial tourist industry has been repeatedly buffeted by regional events, and most people have experienced a fall in income in the last decade. Fewer Jordanians now work abroad (most were in the Arabian Gulf); their remittances back to Jordan were halved after the Gulf crisis, when some 380,000, mainly Palestinians, were forced to return home (MacFarquhar; Viorst, 42).

Jordan's economy is based on tourism, mining, industry, trade, and agriculture. The official unemployment rate is 16 percent, but it is probably twice that. The new king has negotiated a free-trade agreement with the United States and aspires to join the World Trade Organization. He is promoting democratic reforms, freedom of the press, and women's rights (Wright 2001). Much of the workforce is employed by the government and the armed forces.

Jordan's education system is excellent, and its literacy rate had climbed to 87 percent by 1998. It also has an excellent nationwide health program, so the standard of living is relatively high. Jordanians all speak Arabic, and many speak English as their second language.

Ninety-two percent of the Jordanians are Sunni Muslims, 6 percent are Christians, and 2 percent are Shiites or Druze. All groups are tolerant of each other; religion is not a divisive factor in society. Jordanian women are well educated and work in a wide array of fields, mainly teaching, nursing, and clerical work.

Jordanians are very personable, warm, and welcoming. They enjoy friendships with foreigners.

Iraq

What can be said about Iraq? Like Syria, it has a proud history and a long tradition of magnificent civilizations, but time after time, Iraq was beset by invasions and conquests. Unlike heavily populated Egypt, Iraq (Mesopotamia) is underpopulated—about 23 million—although its land is as fertile and its history as old as Egypt's, a consequence of repeated wars and devastation. Iraq's location has made it a strategic battlefield in the region.

Over 75 percent of the Iraqis are Arabs, and 20 percent are Kurds, who are bilingual in Arabic and Kurdish. The remainder are minority ethnic groups: Turkomans, Assyrians, Armenians, and some peoples of Iranian origin. Arabic is the official language, and English is widely spoken by the educated. Ninety-seven percent of the Iraqis are Muslim, of whom 60 percent are Shiite; 3 percent are Christians. Only about 400 of the 150,000 Jews who once lived there remain (Lamb 1995). Iraq has been strongly influenced by its Islamic heritage because several sites sacred to Shiite Muslims are located there and have long been the object of religious pilgrimages.

Iraq's revolutionary socialist government was established after the Hashemite monarchy was overthrown in 1958, and there have been four coups since then. The present authoritarian government has been in power since 1968 and continues to be a serious threat to other nations' interests in the Arabian Gulf area. Social and political influence are limited to a very small elite.

Most recently, of course, Iraq has suffered the catastrophic effects of the 1991 Gulf War. An international embargo was imposed in 1991, which has dealt a serious blow to the economy and to social services. The sale of oil, which in the past provided 95 percent of foreign exchange earnings, dropped to less than 10 percent of previous levels. Prior to the embargo, Iraq boasted a 95 percent literacy rate, 22 universities, the finest health-care system in the Middle East, and a low infant mortality rate.

The embargo changed all this, hitting the flourishing middle class especially hard. What little enters the country by way of consumer goods, food, and medical supplies is diverted by the government to its own loyalists. By 2001 an estimated 800,000 to 1.2 million people had died because of the embargo, half a million of them children under age five (Evans 1997), and 25 percent of Iraq's children are malnourished (this number is up 73 percent since 1990).† Infant mortality for the years 1994 to 1997 was more than double the rate from 1984 to 1989; in 2001 it was about 60 per 1,000 births (as compared with 4 to 5 in Western Europe and 6.7 in the United States).

Enrollments in primary schools dropped from 100 percent in 1980 to 85 percent in 1996; secondary school enrollments declined from 57 percent to 42 percent in the same period. Male literacy fell from 90 percent to about 64 percent, and female literacy was only 43 percent in 1998. Because of scarcities, the people have become even more dependent on the

---

† The death figures are disputed. See Welch 2002.

government for necessities, including drinking water (Greenhut 1998). The currency is almost worthless, and unemployment is about 50 percent (*Middle East Review*, 65).

Since December 1999, when the United Nations Security Council permitted Iraq to export oil to meet humanitarian needs, conditions have improved somewhat. Oil exports are now back to about 75 percent of the pre-Gulf War level.

Iraqi women have always been among the most liberated in the Middle East and are thoroughly integrated into the workforce as professionals and in the fields of education and health care. Women are also active in literature and the arts.

The government has established development projects in agriculture and industry, but these have been overtaken by political activities and priorities. Excellent public health programs were also implemented, but they are severely curtailed now. These initiatives began to suffer during the eight-year war with Iran from 1980 to 1988, and of course the Gulf War was a severe drain on resources. Only 12 percent of the land is cultivated, and efforts have long been under way to reclaim more (it was irrigated and fertile in ancient times). About 30 percent of the Iraqis work in agriculture.

Iraq is now a pariah state and is accused of supporting international terrorism and harboring chemical/biological weapons. This is a country that once had one of the highest living standards in the Middle East. It was an outstanding, cosmopolitan center of culture, art, and intellect. No longer.

Saudi Arabia

Saudi Arabia is a relatively new nation with a large area, mostly desert, and a population of 21 million (up from 14 million since 1992, a growth rate of 3.4 percent annually). Prior to its unification in 1935 by King Abdel-Aziz Ibn Saud, the region that is now Saudi Arabia was loosely governed and inhabited by numerous Bedouin tribes. The Hashemites controlled the west coast region, the Hejaz, with its port of

Jeddah, and its holy cities, Mecca and Medina (Ibn Saud conquered the Hejaz in 1924). King Ibn Saud's descendants still rule. Saudi Arabia has evolved into a viable nation, and the people have a Saudi identity.

Two important elements influence Saudi society: the fact that Arabia was the birthplace of Islam and the discovery of oil, which led to sudden wealth. Religiosity, conservatism, wealth, and foreign workers—all of these factors are present in Saudi Arabia and result in ever-changing attitudes and social policies.

Muslim pilgrimages to the holy cities of Mecca and Medina, throughout the year and especially at the annual Hajj season, are a significant source of income and prestige for the nation; one of the king's titles is "Keeper of the Two Holy Mosques." During the Hajj, the entire country is filled with millions of Muslims from all over the world; there are special airports, camping areas, and health facilities. Saudi Arabia is often called the Holy Land; its Islamic history is central to its identity.

Although oil was first produced in 1938, the real effects of wealth weren't felt until the 1960s and 1970s. It is less wealthy now but is still far better-off than most nations. The Saudis' immense wealth has made them influential in the Arab World, and they are in the forefront of efforts to promote pan-Arabism and pan-Islam. Saudis own many influential newspapers and broadcasting companies (Franklin 1996, 49). They are very concerned with promoting modernization, within the values of conservative Islam; the efforts of modernizers are constantly balanced by demands from religious authorities.

All Saudis are Muslims (in fact, the practice of any other religion is forbidden), and almost all are Sunnis. About 8 percent of the total population are Shiites, 250,000 to 500,000 of whom live on the oil-rich east coast (the king met with leaders of the Shiite community for the first time in 1993) (Murphy 1993; Lancaster 1996; Esposito 1999, 19). All Saudis speak Arabic; Arabia is, after all, where the Arabic language originated. English is widely spoken as a second language.

Saudis follow the Wahhabi sect, a highly rigid and puritanical version of Sunni Islam, practiced elsewhere only in Qatar and for a few years in Afghanistan. "Religious police" regulate attendance at prayer and the closing of shops at prayer times. Restrictions are enforced for citizens and foreigners alike, such as the manner of dress, the prohibition of alcohol, socializing between men and women, control of the media, public entertainment, and the ban on other religions. Saudi Arabia is by far the most authoritarian of the Arab countries, and penalties for noncompliance are severe. Even Arabs and Muslims from other countries need time to adjust after they arrive.

In the 1970s and early 1980s, there were at least five million foreign workers in Saudi Arabia, both laborers and professionals, many of whom came from Arab countries, South Asia, and the Far East; thousands of Westerners from Europe and America also worked there. Foreigners are fewer in number now because the Saudi government is making a concerted effort to replace them with Saudis, especially in management and professional positions. Even now, though, two-thirds of the workforce are foreigners (Schneider 1999). The common laborers, who are mostly non-Western, are likely to remain indefinitely, given the traditional Saudi aversion to manual work. Young university graduates, who were once assured of good positions, are finding jobs and upward mobility far less certain; national income has fallen drastically since the heyday of the 1970s. In fact Saudi Arabia is now struggling through an economic recession, and many public projects are being curtailed. Oil prices fell by over 80 percent between 1982 and 1999. Personal income fell from $19,000 in 1981 to $7,300 in early 2002 (Friedman 2002a). Unemployment is about 20 percent. In December 2001 the government announced that it was cutting spending 20 percent in the next year (Reed 2001).

Saudi Arabia is a welfare state, although some subsidies are shrinking. All adult Saudis, if not independently wealthy, are entitled to a plot of land and a loan of $80,000 to build a home (*The Middle East and North Africa 2001*, 1029).

Health and education programs first instituted in the 1960s have achieved far-reaching results. Life expectancy rose from 40 to 68 in two generations (1955–2000) (*World Population Prospects* 1999, 358). Money has been lavished on public health facilities (there are 318 public and private hospitals), specialized medical care, adult education, and schooling through the university level (there are eight universities); all these are free of charge (Saudi Arabia Information Resource 2001). Population grew so quickly (4.7 percent per year between 1980 and 1997) that 42 percent of the population are under age 14; just under 60 percent are under age 18. The literacy rate is 83 percent for men and 64 percent for women.

The class system of Saudi Arabia is four-tiered: royalty (8,000 princes and 40,000 other members of the royal family) (Kaiser 2002), a growing educated elite, an expanding middle class, and a lower, uneducated class. The latter may be poor, but just as often they are simply isolated from social services and live in their traditional manner. Saudi Arabia is now 83 percent urban, whereas in 1950, about half of the people were still nomadic (Metz 1993, 62).

There are several dissident Islamist (fundamentalist) factions in Saudi Arabia that oppose the rule of the royal family and want to impose even stricter Islamic law, ruling through an "Islamic state." Bin Laden's group is one of these. Fundamentalists have been influential for some time; in November of 1979 Islamic zealots briefly seized and occupied the Great Mosque in Mecca and had to be removed by military force.

Saudi Arabia has the most severe restrictions on women in the entire Middle East (not counting the short-lived Taliban regime in Afghanistan). Women are fully veiled in public, in a long black cloak; they may not travel alone or leave the country without permission from male relatives, nor may they drive cars. In December 2001, women were issued separate ID cards, so now they finally have a fully legal identity (Pope 2002). Few work outside the home; those who do, work in all-female environments such as schools, universities, and even "women's banks" (this ban is eased for health workers) (Abu-Nasr 2000). Between 1990 and 1998, the number of women in the workforce increased from 8 percent to 15 percent, and in 1999 an effort was begun to engage more women in "nation-building" (Al-Khereji 1999). Today, 54 percent of the university students are women (up from a total of 70 women in 1965), and women's enrollment in technical schools rose tenfold between 1994 and 2001 (Pope). Many Saudi women own their own businesses, often computing companies and retail stories. In Jeddah, one fourth of the private businesses are owned by women (Pope).

Saudis are reserved and private, not quick to welcome foreigners into their private lives. Once a friendship is established, however, Saudis are generous and hospitable in the time-honored Arab way.

Yemen

Yemen, long isolated from outside contact and influences, is one of the most colorful and tradition-oriented countries in the Arab World. In ancient times it was called Arabia Felix by the Romans and was known as the main source of incense. Most Yemenis still have strong tribal ties. Social practices have changed relatively slowly since modernization programs were introduced in the late 1960s. Many of Yemen's 18 million people live in remote villages. Yemen's architecture is traditional and distinctive, mainly stone-mud high-rise buildings decorated with white geometric designs.

For three hundred years Yemen was divided into two separate nations—North Yemen and South Yemen (formerly Aden). Yemen's king was deposed in 1962; in the north, the current regime has been in power since 1976; Aden was ruled by pro-Soviet Marxists beginning in 1971. In 1990 the two countries were united under a broadly socialist government. Since the union, however, numerous clashes have occurred, including a civil war in mid-1994, when the south tried to break away from the north. The government's control over many rural areas remains limited, and an uneasy peace currently prevails. There are still social and political tensions left from the long north-south civil war which began in 1972; yet, in 1993 Yemen conducted the only fully free elections ever held in the Arabian Peninsula (Pugh 1993b).

Yemenis are Muslim Arabs. In the north, the most distinctive division is between Sunni Muslims and the Zaidi (Shiite) sect, which dates to the thirteenth century; each group has well-defined geographic boundaries. In the south almost all of the people are Sunni and have intermarried extensively with African and Indian peoples.

Yemenis speak Arabic, including some unusual, isolated dialects in remote areas, and educated Yemenis speak English as a second language. Yemeni men wear distinctive dress: a saronglike skirt and a wide belt in which they place a traditional "jambiyya" dagger.

High mountains and a temperate climate in northern Yemen have made intensive agriculture possible, much of it on terraced land. Coffee and cotton are major sources of revenue. Traditional skills include construction and stone masonry (Yemenis work on construction projects all over the Arabian Peninsula), carpentry, and metalworking. Before the Gulf War many thousands of Yemenis worked elsewhere, and their wages were important to Yemen's economy. After the war, however, Saudi Arabia expelled over one million Yemeni workers (the Yemeni government supported Iraq), with severe economic consequences. Yemen's great hope for the future is oil, first exported in 1993 (Pugh 1993). Oil provides 80 percent of Yemen's earnings, although production dropped by half in 1998. The poverty rate rose from 19 percent in 1992 to 27 percent in 1998.

Unemployment was estimated at 30 percent in 1995. Productivity and prosperity are also affected by the social custom (mostly among men) of chewing a mildly euphoria-producing leaf called *Qat*, beginning in early afternoon every day. Much fertile land is devoted to growing this plant.

Southern Yemen has a semiarid climate, and the people have traditionally been fishermen and merchants (in the coastal area) as well as farmers and herders. The south's geographical location has been advantageous for commerce with countries of the Indian Ocean. A large share of the south's income derives from the procurement and distribution of petroleum products.

Health programs are growing; nonetheless, infant mortality is still very high (68.5 per 1,000 births) and life expectancy is only age 54. In general sanitation is poor and awareness of general health practices nonexistent. Health care is also hampered by a severe shortage of qualified practitioners, particularly in rural areas.

Most of the children now attend school, and the literacy rate has risen to 38 percent (it is only 10 percent among rural women) (Pearl 1997). The government has launched a crash education program (including adults), emphasizing science, engineering, and technology. Forty-eight percent of the population is under age 14.

Women in northern Yemen are fully veiled in public and many are uneducated, yet 29 percent work outside the home owing to financial necessity. Women voted in national elections in 1993, the first women in the Arabian Peninsula to do so; their participation was enthusiastically supported by tribal leaders and by the Islamist political party. An effort is now under way to elect women to parliament (Pearl). In south Yemen, formerly Aden, women were granted equal status by law under the then-Marxist government (the only communist government in the Middle East) and were recruited into the labor force in fields such as accounting and mechanics, or in factories. The women of south Yemen are more integrated into society than in any other Arabian Peninsula country.

Yemenis are admired for their industriousness and skills. They are friendly and curious about the outside world and are very accommodating to foreigners.

Kuwait

Although Kuwait is small, it is an influential country, mostly because of its vast oil wealth, the basis of its economic and political influence among the Arab states. It became independent of British protectorate status in 1961 and has since been ruled by the Al Sabah royal family. Kuwait has had a national assembly and parliamentary elections off and on since 1962 (most recently in 1996). Power lies in the hands of the emir. There is a strong, although relatively moderate, Islamist presence in the parliament (Daniszewski 1996).

In many ways Kuwaiti society resembles that of Saudi Arabia. Both are tribal, religious, and conservative, and the two countries have long had close ties. Kuwaitis are Arab Muslims; about 65 percent are Sunni and 35 percent are Shiites. Their practice of Islam is not, however, as austere as that of Saudi Arabia, although alcohol is banned.

The population of Kuwait is only slightly more than two million—800,000 citizens and about 1.4 million foreigners—but there is a high rate of population growth. So many foreign workers have come to Kuwait that they once constituted 80 percent of the workforce. Many Palestinians and others were forced to leave after the Gulf War of 1991, and since then the emphasis has been on replacing foreign workers with Kuwaitis in professional and managerial jobs. Even so, 70 percent of the workforce was foreign in 1999.

The dominant fact of life in Kuwait is the government's enormous oil-based wealth. Per capita income is one of the highest in the world, although it has dropped slightly. Production of oil began in 1946, and within fifteen years poverty was virtually eradicated (Mansfield 1981, 112). Like Saudi

Arabia, Kuwait is a welfare state. It also has the reputation of being the shrewdest and most sophisticated of the major Arab overseas investors (116).

Another factor that will dominate Kuwaiti affairs for many years is the Iraqi invasion of 1990, followed by the Gulf War. Although the economic effects have largely been overcome, the psychological consequences will last for some time. Kuwaitis have begun reassessing their role as a nation, especially vis-a-vis the rest of the Arab World.

Class distinctions and class consciousness are strong in Kuwait, even as wealth has become more widespread. Progress in health, education, and economic development has completely changed the Kuwaiti way of life over the last fifty years. The literacy rate is 79 percent, and life expectancy is age 77, the highest in the Arab World. The people have everything money can buy. Seventy-five percent of the potable water is distilled or imported, an expenditure impossible for governments with less money and more people.

Kuwaiti women are generally veiled in public, although this is changing. Many are active in education and commerce; some own their own businesses. Unlike Saudi Arabia, Kuwait does not have a prohibition against women working in the same environment as men. The reality that women still do not have the vote (the government approved, but the fundamentalists objected) is a very sensitive issue; women are allowed to drive, however.

Kuwaitis are helpful to foreigners but not quick to establish strong personal friendships. They prefer private and family social circles.

The Arabian Gulf States

The Arabian Gulf (Persian Gulf) states considered together here include Bahrain, Qatar, the United Arab Emirates (UAE), and Oman. They are situated on the eastern coast of the

Arabian Peninsula and were, until 1971, called the Trucial States and under British administration. Many British citizens still live there.

This entire region (including Iraq, Kuwait, Saudi Arabia, Iran, and the Gulf states) has the world's largest oil and natural gas reserves. The Gulf states are very prosperous and are changing rapidly. All but Oman are quite small and lacking in natural resources; their traditional source of income had been trade, fishing, pearling, and piracy. Now, oil revenue dominates everything. These nations have conservative, traditional societies.

Bahrain. Bahrain, an island in the Arabian Gulf, is the most modernized of the Gulf states and was the first to produce oil. Its oil revenues, however, are small (and declining) compared with neighboring states. The government has diversified into dry-dock ship services, aluminum production, and light engineering. Bahrain is an important banking center and also has excellent tourist facilities. It is considered pro-Western and has both a large U.S. naval facility and a British air base.

Bahrainis are Arab Muslims, about 70 percent Shiite and 30 percent Sunni. The emir and his family are Sunni, a cause for concern about future political stability. Bahrain's population of 600,000 comprises 350,000 citizens and 250,000 foreigners. Approximately half of the people live in the capital city of Manama. Arabic is the official language, and English is widely used as a second language.

Bahrain is a constitutional monarchy; elections for one branch of the bicameral legislature will be held in October 2002 (Schneider 2002). Women were given the right to vote in March 2002 (Reuters 2002).

Bahrain's small size and population have contributed to its rapid modernization. Education and health programs are universal, and the literacy rate is 86 percent. Many Bahraini women are well educated, and the majority of those who hold college degrees are working; they constitute 19 percent of the workforce. Bahrain is not without social problems, however; there are tensions between the Sunni government and its Shiite citizens, and unemployment is over 30 percent among the Shiite population.

Qatar. Qatar is a peninsula, fabulously rich in both oil and natural gas, and it offers great employment and commercial opportunities. Since the discovery of oil in 1949, Qatar's population has more than doubled, and approximately 75 percent of the workforce are foreigners. Indigenous Qataris numbered 350,000 in 1991 and 506,000 ten years later, in 2001. About 80 percent of the population live in the capital city of Doha. Almost everything is imported.

Until the discovery of oil, the Qatari people were engaged in fishing, pearling, and trading, many living in dire poverty. Now their lives are being rapidly transformed by education and health programs and by state subsidies. The literacy rate is 79 percent, and life expectancy is age 74. Qatar had the phenomenal growth rate of 6.1 percent between 1990 and 1998; half of the people are under age 15.

The Qataris are Arab Muslims; they speak Arabic and use English as their second language. The country is ruled by an emir, and the society is very conservative; it is the only other country that follows the same puritanical Wahhabi sect of Islam as Saudi Arabia (but without as many official restrictions). The country is so small that the emir runs the government like a family business and rules in conjunction with an advisory council. The government is generally pro-Western. A Lebanese-American Muslim woman has been retained by the government as an adviser to draft Qatar's Personal Status Code (women's rights and family law).

Qatar has recently become known for its television channel Al Jazeera, which is widely watched all over the world and has been a source of information about the Al Qaeda organization of Bin Laden. Qatar permits freedom of the press, and an initiative to set up an Islamic satellite channel in several languages is under way, one purpose of which is to rectify incorrect information about Islam and Muslims (Hassan 2001).

Qatar's social organization is still tribal and strongly family-oriented. Although its educated young men are beginning to assume professional and managerial positions, Qatari women are not yet very active in the workforce; they constitute about 12 percent. They will, however, have the right to vote in parliamentary elections scheduled for 2003 (Beyer).

United Arab Emirates. The United Arab Emirates is a federation of small territories that was created in 1971–1972 by uniting seven of the Trucial States. Its combined population is about 2.4 million. Abu Dhabi is the largest of the former territories, and is the capital; Dubai is the main port and commercial center as well as a major airport hub. The population is 85 percent urban.

The union has worked out well on the whole, and rulers of the smaller areas realize that they have attained a larger degree of influence and economic benefit through alliance with their larger neighbors than would have been possible otherwise. The people are Arab Muslims, of whom about 80 percent are Sunni and 20 percent are Shiite. All seven states are ruled by Sunnis.

Abu Dhabi began oil production in 1962, Dubai in 1969, and Sharjah in 1973 (Niblock 1980, 13). Life has been transformed—former fishing villages are now modern cities filled with high-rise buildings and superhighways. The other four small emirates, each with a small population, have no oil and are changing more slowly. Dubai has become a huge, prosperous commercial hub for the whole Gulf region. Per capita income is the second highest in the Gulf. About 80 percent of the residents are foreigners.

Since the present ruler took power in 1966, ambitious programs have been established in education, health, and agricultural production. Literacy is 79 percent, and life expectancy is 75 years. The society is still very traditional and conservative, and women are veiled and participate little in public life; this is changing, however, now that women's education through the university level is strongly encouraged by the government.

Oman. Oman is not as wealthy as the other Gulf countries, and it is quite large in area. It is geographically strategic because of its location on the Strait of Hormuz at the entrance to the Arabian Gulf. Oman is ruled by a sultan, from the family that has ruled since 1744 (after gaining its independence from Iran).

Oman's population is about 2.6 million, of whom 20 percent are foreigners (over half of them from the Indian subcontinent and other parts of Asia). Eighty-five percent of the population are Arabs, and the rest are of Zanzibari, Baluchi, or South Asian origin. Almost all of the people speak Arabic; some non-Arabic Semitic languages are still spoken in the far south. About 70 percent of the Omanis are of the Ibadi sect (a branch of Shiism), which has contributed to an isolationist tendency. Twenty-five percent are Sunnis, and the rest are Shiites, who usually live in their own communities. The principal non-Muslim minority group is Indian Hindus, who have resided in Oman for centuries.

Tribalism is still the main source of identity for the Omani people. The discovery of oil in 1967 has led to rapid modernization and social change; still, the nation is not wealthy. Seventy percent of the national income is from oil; oasis agriculture is also important, and now the remote interior settlements have more contact with the rest of the country. In 1998, 81 percent of the people lived in urban areas.

Although Oman has a considerable amount of potentially arable land, it lacks manpower and water. But life is getting better, phenomenally better. Literacy was 67 percent in 1998, and improved health-care practices resulted in a 3.4 percent population growth between 1992 and 1998. The indigenous population of Oman tripled between 1965 and 1990 (Range

1995, 112–38). Electricity, telephones, radio, television, public education, roads, hospitals, public health programs—all are new since the present sultan took power in 1970.

Oman's sultan is known to be one of the most innovative rulers in the Gulf. He opposes Islamic fundamentalism and promotes widespread education and computer training. His goal is a 90 percent Omani workforce by 2010 (Daniszewski 1999). Oman joined the World Trade Organization in November of 2000.

Omani women have traditionally had a small role in society, but this is changing as the sultan continues to revolutionize their lives. In 1996, 65 percent of the students in Oman's national university were women, and they will soon have a significant role in the workplace. He appointed the first female ambassador from an Arab country (Daniszewski). There are two elected women in parliament and two on the sultan's Consultative Council (Al-Hibri 1999).

Appendix C

The Arabic Language

Learning Arabic is indispensable for gaining a real insight into Arab society and culture. If you intend to study Arabic, you should choose the type that suits your own needs best.

Arabs associate foreign learners of Arabic with scholars, who (in the past) have tended to concentrate on Classical Arabic, so if you ask an Arab to give you lessons in Arabic, he or she will usually want to start with the alphabet and emphasize reading. If your interest is mainly in learning spoken Arabic, you will have to make that clear from the outset.

When you speak Arabic, you will find that your use of even the simplest phrases, no matter how poorly pronounced, will produce an immediate smile and comment of appreciation. I have had literally hundreds of occasions on which my willingness to converse in Arabic led to a delightful experience. A typical example occurred once when I was shopping in a small town in Lebanon and spent about half an hour chatting with the owner of one of the shops. When I was about to leave, he insisted on giving me a small brass camel, "because you speak Arabic."

Arabs are flattered by your efforts to learn their language (although they are convinced that no foreigner can ever master it), and they will do everything to encourage you. Even just a little Arabic is a useful tool for forming friendships and demonstrating goodwill.

Colloquial Arabic Dialects

The Arabic dialects fall into five geographical categories:

Category	Dialects	Native or Other Language Influence
1. North African (Western Arabic)	Moroccan Algerian Tunisian Libyan Mauretanian	Berber
2. Egyptian/Sudanese	Egyptian Sudanese	Turkish, Coptic, Nilotic
3. Levantine*	Lebanese Syrian Jordanian Palestinian	Local Semitic languages (Aramaic, Phoenician, Canaanite)
4. Arabian Peninsular	Saudi Yemeni Kuwaiti Gulf (Bahrain, Qatar, the Emirates) Omani	Farsi (in the Gulf states), Bedouin dialects, South Arabian languages
5. Iraqi†	Iraqi	Local Semitic languages (Assyrian, Chaldean), Farsi, Turkish

---

* The term *Levantine* is derived from the French name for the area bordering the eastern Mediterranean. This area (especially Lebanon and Syria) is referred to as the "Levant" in French and English.

† Iraqi is essentially a nonurban dialect, with three distinct varieties, similar to both Jordanian and Kuwaiti Arabic.

Speakers of dialects in three of the categories—Egyptian/
Sudanese, Levantine, and Arabian Peninsular—have relatively little difficulty understanding each other. The North
African, Iraqi, and Gulf dialects, however, are relatively difficult for other Arabs to understand.

The most noticeable differences among dialects occur in
the vocabulary, although there are grammatical discrepancies
too. These variations should be taken into account when you
are choosing a dialect to study, since it is almost useless to
study a dialect different from the one spoken in the country
to which you are going.

Simple words and phrases, such as greetings, vary widely,
while technical and erudite words are usually the same. Educated Arabs get around this problem by using classical words,
but a foreigner is more likely to experience each dialect as a
different language. The following are examples of differences
among dialects.

Slightly Different

	Egyptian	Saudi	Moroccan
paper	wara'a	waraga	werqa

	Jordanian	Moroccan	Egyptian
beautiful	jameela	jmila	gameela

	Saudi	Tunisian	Lebanese
heavy	tageel	thaqeel	ti'eel

Completely Different

	Lebanese	Egyptian	Iraqi	Tunisian
How are you?	keefak?	izzayyak?	shlownak?	shniyya hwalak?

	Moroccan	Egyptian	Jordanian	Saudi
now	daba	dilwa'ti	halla'	daheen

	Lebanese	Kuwaiti	Moroccan	Egyptian
good	mneeh	zayn	mezyan	kwayyis

Attitudes toward Dialects

Arabs tend to regard their own dialect as the purest and the closest to Classical Arabic; I have heard this claim vigorously defended from Morocco to Iraq. In fact, though, where one dialect is closer to the Classical with respect to one feature, another dialect is closer with respect to another. No dialect can be successfully defended as pure except possibly the Najdi dialect spoken in central Arabia, which has been the most isolated from non-Arabic influences.

Arabs view the Bedouin dialects as semiclassical and therefore admirable, although a bit archaic. Most Arabs find the Egyptian dialect to be the most pleasing to listen to because the pronunciation is "light." Eastern Arabs tend to look down on western Arabic (North African) because of their difficulty in understanding the dialect (which they attribute, wrongly, to Berber usages). Most of the differences between western and eastern Arabic stem from changes in pronunciation and word stress.

Because all Arabs view their local dialect as the best, they are quick to advise a foreigner that theirs is the most useful, but usefulness depends entirely on where you are in the Arab World.

The Structure of Arabic

The structure of Arabic is like that of all Semitic languages. Its most striking feature is the way words are formed, which is called the "root and pattern" system. A root is a set of three consonants that carry the meaning of the word. The vowels in a word form patterns and, depending on how they are intermixed with the consonants, determine the part of speech of a word. The consonants and vowels have different functions in a word, and together, their combinations yield a rich vocabulary. Here are some examples from Classical Arabic, distinguishing roots and patterns (patterns may contain affixes—additional syllables added at the beginning, in the middle, or at the end of words).

		Meaning
Roots:	k-t-b	writing
	r-k-b	riding
Patterns:	-a-(a)-a (i)	(completed action, past tense)
	-aa-i-	agent (one who does an action)
	ma—a-	place (where the action is done)
Words:	*kataba*	he wrote
	rakiba	he rode
	kaatib	writer, clerk
	raakib	rider
	maktab	(place for writing) office, desk
	markab	(place for riding) boat
	markaba	vehicle

As you learn vocabulary, you will notice that words that have the same core meaning come in varying patterns, but almost all can be reduced to a three-consonant base. For example, other words that share the consonants *k-t-b* are

kitaab	book
kitaaba	writing
maktaba	library, bookstore
maktuub	letter, something written, fate

Personal names in Arabic usually have a meaning. Below is a group of names from the same three-consonant base, *h-m-d*, which means "to praise":

Muhammad	Hamdy
Mahmoud	Hammady
Hameed	Hamoud
Hamed	Ahmed

You can see why foreigners sometimes find Arabic names confusing!

Arabic pronunciation makes use of many sounds that do not occur in English, mostly consonants produced far back in the mouth and throat. Some of these consonants show up in the English spelling of words, such as *gh* (Baghdad), *kh* (Khartoum), *q* (Qatar), and *dh* (Riyadh).

In Classical Arabic there are twenty-eight consonants, three long vowels, and three short vowels. In the Arabic dialects, some consonants have been dropped or merged with others, and some consonants and vowels have been added—features which distinguish one dialect from another.

Arabic Writing

The Arabic alphabet has twenty-eight letters and is written from right to left. Numerals, however, are written from left to right. Most letters connect with the preceding and following letters in the same word. Sometimes two or three sounds are written using the same letter; in this case they are differentiated from each other by the arrangement of dots, for example:

b ب	r ر	s س
t ت	z ز	sh ش
th ث		

Because consonants carry the meaning of words, the Arabic alphabet (like all Semitic alphabets) includes only the consonants and the long vowels (for example, *aa*, which is a different vowel from *a* and is held longer when pronounced). The short vowels do not appear in the alphabet, but the Arab reader knows what they are and can pronounce the words correctly because these vowels come in predictable patterns. Additional signs (diacritical marks) mark short vowels, doubled consonants, and the like, but these are used only in texts for beginners—and are always included in the text of the Qur'an in order to assure correct reading.

The numerals in Arabic are very easy to learn. We refer to our own numbers as "Arabic numerals" because the system of using one symbol for 0 through 9 and adding new place values for tens, hundreds, and so forth, was borrowed from the Arabs to replace the Roman numeral system. Nevertheless, although their numerals are used the same way as ours, they are not alike (note especially their numbers 5 and 6, which look like our 0 and 7).

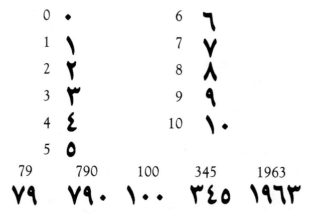

There are several styles of handwriting, and in each the shapes of the individual letters are slightly different. The difference between North African or western script, for instance, and eastern script is especially noticeable.

Calligraphy As an Art Form

Decorative calligraphy, as you might guess, is one of the highest artistic expressions of Arab culture. Most letters of the alphabet are full of flowing curves, so an artist can easily form them into elaborate designs. Calligraphy usually depicts Qur'anic quotations or favorite proverbs, and the patterns are often beautifully balanced and intricate. Calligraphic designs are widely used to decorate mosques, monuments, books, and household items such as brass trays.

Calligraphy and arabesque geometric designs have developed because of the Islamic injunction against paintings and statues in places of worship. This emphasis is very evident in Islamic architecture.

Social Greetings

Arabs use many beautiful, elaborate greetings and blessings—and in every type of situation. Most of these expressions are predictable—each situation calls for its own statements and responses.

Situational expressions exist in English, but they are few, such as "How are you?"/"Fine," "Thank you"/"You're welcome," and "Have a nice day." In Arabic there are at least thirty situations that call for predetermined expressions. Although these are burdensome for a student of Arabic to memorize, it is comforting to know that you can feel secure about what to say in almost every social context.

There are formulas for greetings in the morning and evening, for meeting after a long absence, for meeting for the first time, and for welcoming someone who has returned from a trip. There are formulas for acknowledging accomplishments, purchases, marriage, or death and for expressing good wishes when someone is drinking a glass of water, is engaged in a task, or has just had a haircut! All of these situations have required responses, and they are beautiful in delivery and usually religious in content. Some examples follow.

English (Statement/Response)	Arabic Translation (Statement/Response)
Good morning./Good morning.	Morning of goodness./Morning of light.
Good-bye./Good-bye.	[Go] with safety./May God make you safe.

Happy to see you back./Thanks.	Thanks be to God for your safety./May God make you safe.
(Said when someone is working)	God give you strength./ God strengthen you.
(Said when discussing future plans)	May our Lord make it easy.
Good night./Good night.	May you reach morning in goodness./And may you be of the same group.
I'm taking a trip. What can I bring you?/What would you like?	Your safety.
I have news. Guess what I heard.	[May it be] good, God willing.

Conversational ritual expressions are much used in Arabic. Sometimes a ritual exchange of formalities can last five or ten minutes, particularly among older and more traditional people.

The Arabs have the charming custom of addressing strangers with kinship terms, which connotes respect and goodwill at the same time. One Western writer was struck by the use of these terms with strangers in Yemeni society (they are as widely used elsewhere).

"Brother, how can I help you?"
"Take this taxi, my sisters, I'll find another."
"My mother, it's the best that I can do."
"You're right, uncle." (Mandaville 1981, 30)

Ritualistic statements are required by etiquette in many situations. Meeting someone's small child calls for praise carefully mixed with blessings; for example, "May God keep him" or "[This is] what God wills." Such statements reassure the parents that you are not envious (you certainly would not add, "I wish I had a child like this!"). Blessings should also be used when seeing something of value, such as a new car

("May you drive it safely") or a new house ("May you live here happily"). When someone purchases something, even a rather small item, the usual word is *Mabrook*, which is translated "Congratulations" but literally means "Blessed." Some of the most common phrases are given here.

English	*Arabic*
Hello./Hello.	*Marhaba./Marhabtayn.*
Good morning./Good morning.	*Sabah alkhayr./Sabah annoor.*
Peace be upon you./And upon you peace.	*Assalamu 'alaykum./Wa 'alaykum assalam.*
Good-bye./Good-bye. ([Go] with safety./May God make you safe.)	*Ma'a ssalama./Allah yisallimak.*
Thank you./You're welcome.	*Shukran./'Afwan.*
Congratulations./Thank you. (Blessed./May God bless you.)	*Mabrook./Allah yibarik feek.*
Welcome./Thanks. (Welcome./Welcome to you.)	*Ahlan wa sahlan./Ahlan beek.*
If God wills.	*Inshallah.* (Said when speaking of a future event)
What God wills.	*Mashallah.* (Said when seeing a child or complimenting someone's health)
Thanks be to God.	*Alhamdu lillah.*
Thanks be to God for your safety.	*Hamdillah 'ala ssalama.* (Said when someone returns from a trip or recovers from an illness)

Some Arabic expressions sound much too elaborate to be used comfortably in English. There is no need to use them exactly in translation if you are speaking English, as long as you express good wishes.

Bibliography and References

Abdullah, M. Salim. 1995. "Muslims in Germany." In *Muslim Minorities in the West*, edited by Syed Abedin and Ziauddin Sardar. London: Grey Seal.

Abedin, Syed, and Ziauddin Sardar, eds. 1995. *Muslim Minorities in the West*. London: Grey Seal.

Abu-Laban, Baha. 1995. "The Muslim Community of Canada." In *Muslim Minorities in the West*, edited by Syed Abedin and Ziauddin Sardar. London: Grey Seal.

Abumalham, Montserrat. 1996. "The Muslim Presence in Spain." In *Muslims in the Margin: Political Responses to the Presence of Islam in Western Europe*, edited by W. A. R. Shadid and P. S. van Konigsveld. Kampen, The Hague: Kok Pharos Publishing House.

Abu-Nasr, Donna. 2000. "The Veiled Life of Saudi Women." *Washington Post*, 8 December.

"ACLU Challenges Strip Search of Muslim Woman at O'Hare Airport." 2002. U.S. Newswire, 16 January. www.usnewswire.com

Al-Ba'albaki, Munir. 1982. "English Words of Arabic Origin." In *Al-Mawrid, A Modern English-Arabic Dictionary*, 101–12. Beirut: Dar El-Ilm Lil-Malayen.

Algosaibi, Ghazi A. 1982. *Arabian Essays*. London: Kegan Paul International.

Al-Hibri, Azizah. 1999. "Muslim Women's Rights in the Global Village." *American Muslims for Global Peace and Justice Newsletter*, 26 September. www.global peaceandjustice.org

Al-Janadriyya National Heritage and Culture Festival. 1995. Riyadh, 11th session (January). This annual conference brings together a broad array of Arab, European, and American intellectuals.

Al-Khereji, Nourah. 1999. "Religion, Vision Behind Abdullah's Support for Women's Role." *Arab News*, 7 May.

Allen, J. A. 1981. *Libya: The Experience of Oil*. Boulder, CO: Westview Press.

Ammar, Nawal H. 1995. "On Being a Muslim Woman: Laws and Practices." Population Conference, Beijing.

Anderson, Norman. 1976. *Law Reform in the Muslim World*. London: University of London, Athlone Press.

Arab American Institute. 2001. "A Poll of Arab Americans Since the Terrorist Attack on the United States." Washington, DC.

Arab American Institute. 2000. "Arab Americans." Washington, DC.

Arberry, A. J. 1955. *The Koran Interpreted*. New York: Macmillan.

Armstrong, Karen. 2000. *Islam: A Short History*. New York: Modern Library.

Atiyeh, George N., ed. 1977. *Arab and American Cultures*. Washington, DC: American Enterprise Institute for Public Policy Research.

Bagby, Perl, and Froehle Bagby. 2001. *The Mosque in America: A National Portrait*. Washington, DC: Council on American-Islamic Relations.

Bakar, Osman. 1999. *The History and Philosophy of Islamic Science*. Cambridge, England: Islamic Texts Society.

Ballard, Roger. 1996. "Islam and the Construction of Europe." In *Muslims in the Margin: Political Responses to the Presence of Islam in Western Europe*, edited by W. A. R. Shadid and P. S. van Konigsveld. Kampen, The Hague: Kok Pharos Publishing House.

Barakat, Halim. 1993. *The Arab World: Society, Culture, and the State*. Berkeley: University of California Press.

Barakat, Robert A. 1973. "Talking with Hands." *Time*, 17 September, 65–66.

198

Bashir, Abdul Wahab. 2002. "Scholars Define Terrorism, Call for Joint Action to Defend Islam." *Arab News*, 12 January.

Bell, Richard. 1953. *Introduction to the Qur'an*. Edinburgh: University Press.

Beyer, Lisa. 2001. "The Women of Islam." *Time*, 3 December.

Bhutto, Benzair. 1998. "Politics and the Modern Woman." In *Liberal Islam, A Sourcebook*, edited by Charles Kurzman. New York: Oxford Univeristy Press.

"Bias Against Muslims Spreads." 1995. *Orange County Register*. 28 August.

Bin Sultan, Bandar. 1994. "Modernize but Not Westernize." *Washington Post*, 4 July.

Bistofi, Robert. 1995. "Approaches de l'Islam dans l'Union Européenne." In *Islams d'Europe*, edited by Robert Bistofi and François Zabbal, 15–63. Paris: Editions de l'Aube.

Bistofi, Robert, and François Labbal, eds. 1995. *Islams d'Europe*. Paris: Editions de l'Aube.

Blank, Jonah. 1998. "The Muslim Mainstream." *U.S. News and World Report*, 20 July.

Borowiec, Andrew. 1996. "Tunisia Thrives by Looking to Future." *Washington Times*, 13 November.

Boullata, Issa J. 1990. *Trends and Issues in Contemporary Arab Thought*. Albany: State University of New York Press.

Bowen, Donna Lee, and Evelyn A. Early, eds. 1993. *Everyday Life in the Muslim Middle East*. Bloomington: Indiana University Press.

Britannica Book of the Year. 2001. Chicago, Encyclopedia Britannica.

Brown, L. Carl. 2000. *Religion and State*. New York: Columbia University Press.

Brown, L. Carl, and Norman Itzkowitz. 1977. *Psychological Dimensions of Near Eastern Studies*. Princeton: Darwin Press.

Cohn, D'Vera. 2001. "Statistics Portray Settled, Affluent Mideast Community." *Washington Post*, 20 November.

Collelo, Thomas, ed. 1989. *Lebanon: A Country Study*. Washington, DC: Department of the Army.

———, ed. 1988. *Syria: A Country Study*. 3d ed. Washington, DC: Department of the Army.

Condon, John, and Fathi S. Yousef. 1977. "The Middle Eastern Home." In *An Introduction to Intercultural Communication*, 159–62. Indianapolis: Bobbs-Merrill.

Cooperman, Alan. 2002a. "Scholars Plan to Show How Attacks Violated Islamic Law." *Washington Post*, 20 January.

———. 2002b. "Sept. 11 Backlash Murders and the State of 'Hate'." *Washington Post*, 20 January.

Council on American Islamic Relations. www.cair-net.org

Culver, Virginia. 2002. "Many American Muslims Well Off, College Educated, Poll Shows." *Denver Post*, 18 January.

Daniszewski, John. 1999. "The Sultanate's Arabian Knight." *Los Angeles Times*, 15 December.

———. 1997a. "A Ray of Hope in War-Torn Sudan." *New York Times*, 18 October.

———. 1997b. "Mideast Christians Feel Persecuted." *Los Angeles Times*, 14 August.

———. 1996. "Kuwaitis with a Vote Give Voice to Democracy." *Los Angeles Times*, 30 September.

Dawood, N. J. 1964. *The Koran*. New York: Penguin Books.

Dekmejian, R. Hrair. 1995. *Islam in Revolution, Fundamentalism in the Arab World*. 2d ed. Syracuse, NY: Syracuse University Press.

"Delta Apologizes to Muslim Teen Forced to Remove Headscarf." 2002. Council on American Islamic Relations. 17 January. www.cair-net.org

Department of International Economic Affairs. 1989. *Prospects of World Urbanization 1988*, Population Studies no. 112. New York: United Nations.

Diehl, Wilhelm. 1984. *Holy War*. New York: Macmillan.

Dwyer, Claire. 1996. "The Establishment of Islamic Schools." In *Muslims in the Margin: Political Responses to the Presence of Islam in Western Europe*, edited by W.

A. R. Shadid and P. S. van Konigsveld. Kampen, The Hague: Kok Pharos Publishing House.

Edwards, Brian T. 1996. "Tangier Belies Morocco's Stable Image." *Washington Times*, 5 July.

El Guindi, Fadwa. 1981. "Is There an Islamic Alternative? The Case of Egypt's Contemporary Islamic Movement." *International Insight* 1, no. 6 (July/August): 19–24.

Esposito, John L. 1999. *The Islamic Threat, Myth or Reality?* 3d ed. New York: Oxford University Press.

———. 1998a. *Islam and Politics.* 4th ed. Syracuse NY: Syracuse University Press.

———. 1998b. *Islam, The Straight Path.* 3d ed. New York: Oxford University Press.

———, ed. 1995. *Oxford Encyclopedia of the Modern Islamic World.* New York: Oxford University Press.

"Europe Slow to Invest in North Africa." 1993. *Christian Science Monitor*, 27 January.

Evans, Dominic. 1997. "Iraqi Care Worsens as Sanctions' Grip Tightens." *Washington Post*, 30 December.

Faith in Action. Newsletter. 2001. "Muslims Reach Agreement with Dallas Newspaper." Council on American Islamic Relations, Fall. www.cair-net.org

Fazili, Samira. 2001. "Religious Discrimination Against Muslims in Western Europe." Testimony before the U.S. House Committee on International Relations, Subcommittee on Human Rights, 11 July.

Federation of Islamic Organizations in Europe, 2002. www.fioe.org

Fernea, Elizabeth. 2000. "Islamic Feminism Finds a Different Voice." *Foreign Service Journal* (May): 27–30.

Findley, Paul. 2001. *Silent No More: Confronting America's False Image of Islam*. Beltsville, MD: Amana Publications.

Finn, Peter. 2002. "A Turn from Tolerance." *New York Times*, 29 March.

Finnegan, William. 1999. "The Invisible War." *The New Yorker*, 25 January.

Fisher, Ian. 2001. "Europe's Muslims Seek a Path amid Competing Cultures." *New York Times*, 8 December.

Flanigan, James. 2002. "Amid Middle East Strife, A New Focus on Economics." *Los Angeles Times*, 17 March.

Ford, Peter. 2001. "Listening for Islam's Silent Majority." *Christian Science Monitor*, 5 November.

Franklin, Stephen. 1996. "The Kingdom and the Power." *Columbia Journalism Review*, November/December.

Friedman, Thomas. 2002a. "The Saudi Challenge." *Los Angeles Times*, 20 February.

———. 2002b. "The Two Domes of Belgium." *New York Times*, 27 January.

Ghose, Dave. 2002. "Tides of Support Buoy a City's Displaced Muslims." *Christian Science Monitor*, 15 January.

Greenberg, Irving, and Jerome Shestack. 2000. "Carnage in Sudan." *Washington Post*, 31 October.

Greenhut, Steven. 1998. "The Face of Sanctions." *Orange County Register*, 6 December.

Grimsley, Kirstin. 2001. "More Arabs, Muslims Allege Bias on the Job." *Washington Post*, 12 February.

Haddad, Yvonne Y., ed. 2002. *Muslims in the West: From Sojourners to Citizens*. New York: Oxford University Press.

Haddad, Yvonne Y., and John L. Esposito. 1998. *Muslims on the Americanization Path?* New York: Oxford University Press.

Haddad, Yvonne Y. and Jane Smith, eds. 2002. *Muslim Minorities in the West: Visible and Invisible*. New York: Altamira Press.

Hall, Edward T. 1966. *The Hidden Dimension*. New York: Doubleday.

———. 1979. "Learning the Arabs' Silent Language." *Psychology Today* 13, no. 3 (August): 45–54.

Hamady, Sania. 1960. *Temperament and Character of the Arabs*. New York: Twayne.

Hanafi, Hasan. 1992. "Image of the Self and Other." Middle East Studies Association Conference.

Harrington, Kimberly. 2001. "Microfund for Women: Building a Better Future for Women in Jordan." *Jordan Times*, 7 December.

Hassan, Dahi. 2001. "Islamic Satellite Channel Planned." *Gulf News*, 24 December.

Hassan, Riaz. 1995. "Muslim Relations in Australian Society." In *Muslim Minorities in the West*, edited by Syed Abedin and Ziauddin Sardar. London: Grey Seal.

Helicke, James. 2002. "Turks in Germany: Muslim Identity 'Between' States." In *Muslim Minorities in the West: Visible and Invisible*, edited by Yvonne Y. Haddad and Jane Smith. New York: Altamira Press.

"Historical Ties Leave Trying Legacy." 1993. *Christian Science Monitor*, 27 January.

Hjarno, Jan. 1996. "Muslims in Denmark." In *Muslims in the Margin: Political Responses to the Presence of Islam in Western Europe*, edited by W. A. R. Shadid and P. S. van Konigsveld. Kampen, The Hague: Kok Pharos Publishing House.

Hoodbhoy, Pervez. 1991. *Islam and Science*. London: Zed Books.

Hoover, Felix. 2002. "Neighbors Reach Out to Mosque." *Columbus Dispatch*, 1 January.

Hussain, S. S., and S. A. Ashraf, eds. 1979. *Crisis in Muslim Education*. Jeddah: King Abdulaziz University.

Ianari, Vittorio. 1995. "Une demande de dialogue et des elements de conflict." In *Islams d'Europe*, edited by Robert Bistofi and François Zabbal, 322–23. Paris: Editions de l'Aube.

Ignatius, David. 2002. "The Transatlantic Rift Is Getting Serious." *Washington Post*, 15 February.

"Information and Misinformation in Euro-Arab Relations." 1988. The Hague: The Lutfia Rabbani Foundation.

International Action Center. www.iacenter.org

Johns, Anthony, and Abdullah Saeed. 2002. "Muslims in Australia: The Building of a Community." In *Muslim Minorities in the West: Visible and Invisible*, edited by Yvonne Y. Haddad and Jane Smith. New York: Altamira Press.

Kaiser, Robert. 2002. "Enormous Wealth Spilled into American Coffers." *Washington Post*, 11 February.

Kaplan, Roger. 1998. "The Libel of Moral Equivalence." *Atlantic Monthly*, August.

Karim, Karim H. 2002. "Crescent Dawn in the Great White North: Muslim Participation in the Canadian Public Sphere." In *Muslims in the West: From Sojourners to Citizens*, edited by Yvonne Y. Haddad. New York: Oxford University Press.

Khalidi, Ramla, and Judith Tucker. 1991. *Women's Rights in the Arab World*. Washington, DC: Middle East Report.

Khodr, Mohamed. 2001. "America's Media: Israel's Good, Muslims Bad." 14 October. mediamonitors.net

"Kissing Cousins: Marriage among Relatives Set New Records in the Middle East." 1996. *Al Jadid Magazine* 2, no. 5 (March): 9.

Kurzman, Charles, ed. 1998. *Liberal Islam, A Sourcebook*. New York: Oxford University Press.

Laffin, John. 1975. *Rhetoric and Reality, The Arab Mind Considered*. New York: Taplinger Publishing.

Lamb, David. 1995. "In a Region of Hate, Morocco Is the Land of Harmony." *Los Angeles Times*, 25 October.

———. 1987. *The Arabs, Journeys beyond the Mirage*. New York: Random House.

Lampman, Jane. 2002. "Muslim in America." *Christian Science Monitor*, 10 January.

Lancaster, John. 1998. "Hundreds of Algerians Reportedly Burned Alive in Holy Month Scourge." *Washington Post*, 7 January.

———. 1996. "Saudi Tension Could Reignite." *Washington Post*, 1 November.

Lawrence, T. E. 1926. *Seven Pillars of Wisdom*. New York: Doubleday.

Lerch, Wolfgang G. 2001. *Frankfurter Allgemeine Zeitung*, 16 October. Quoted in *World Press Review*, January 2002, 8.

Lewis, Bernard. 2002. "What Went Wrong?" *Atlantic* (January): 44.

Lippman, Thomas. 1990. *Understanding Islam, An Introduction to the Muslim World*. New York: Penguin Books.

MacFarquhar, Neil. 2001. "Syria Reaches Turning Point, But Which Way Will It Turn?" *New York Times*, 12 March.

Maddy-Weitzman, Bruce, ed. 1998. *Middle East Contemporary Survey*. Vol. 22. Boulder, CO: Westview Press.

Mahnig, Hans. 2002. "Islam in Switzerland: Fragmented Accommodation in a Federal Country." In *Muslims in the West: From Sojourners to Citizens*, edited by Yvonne Y. Haddad. New York: Oxford University Press.

Mandaville, Jon. 1981. "Impressions from a Writer's Notebook—At Home in Yemen." *Aramco World* 32, no. 3 (May/June): 30–33.

Mansfield, Peter. 1981. *The New Arabians*. New York: Doubleday.

Marquand, Robert. 1996. "Media Still Portray Muslims as Terrorists." *Christian Science Monitor*, 22 January.

McGrory, Mary. 2002. "'Nuancing' the Mideast Dilemma." *Washington Post*, 14 April.

McLoughlin, Leslie J. 1982. *Colloquial Arabic (Levantine)*. London: Routledge and Kegan Paul.

Melikian, Levon H. 1977. "The Modal Personality of Saudi College Students: A Study in National Character." In *Psychological Dimensions of Near Eastern Studies*, edited by L. Carl Brown and Norman Itzkowitz, 166–209. Princeton: Darwin Press.

Merriam-Webster's Collegiate Dictionary, 10th ed. 1993. Springfield, MA: Merriam-Webster.

Metz, Helen Chapin, ed. 1993. *Saudi Arabia: A Country Study*. 5th ed. Washington, DC: Library of Congress Federal Research Division.

Middle East and North Africa 2001, The. 2001. 47th ed. London: Europa Publications.

Middle East Review. 2000. 25th ed. Essex, UK: World of Information.

Moussalli, Ahmad S. 1999. *Moderate and Radical Islamic Fundamentalism*. Gainesville: University of Florida Press.

Murphy, Caryle. 1993. "Saudi King Reconciles with Shiite Opposition." *Washington Post*, 16 October.

Muslim Public Affairs Council. 2002. www.amila.org

Naguib, Saphinaz-Amal. 2002. "The Northern Way: Muslim Communities in Norway." In *Muslim Minorities in the West: Visible and Invisible*, edited by Yvonne Y. Haddad and Jane Smith. New York: Altamira Press.

Niblock, Tim. 1980. "Introduction." In *Social and Economic Development in the Arab Gulf*, edited by Tim Niblock, 11–19. New York: St. Martin's Press.

Nielsen, Jorgen. 1995. *Muslims in Western Europe*. 2d ed. Edinburgh: Edinburgh University Press.

Nonneman, Gerd, Tim Niblock, and Bogdan Szajkowski, eds. 1996. *Muslim Communities in the New Europe*. Reading, UK: Ithaca Press.

Omran, Abdel R. 1980. *Population in the Arab World: Problems and Prospects.* London: Croom Helm.

Osman, Mohamed. 2002. "U.S. to Mediate Sudan Peace Talks." *Washington Post,* 13 January.

Overbye, Dennis. 2001. "How Islam Won, and Lost, the Lead in Science." *New York Times,* 30 October.

Palumbo, Michael. 1987. *The Palestinian Catastrophe.* London: Faber and Faber.

Pappas, Charles. 2001. "Should American Values Be Marketed to Muslim Nations?" *New York Times,* 17 December.

Patai, Raphael. 1973. *The Arab Mind.* New York: Scribner.

Pearl, Daniel. 1997. "Yemen Steers a Path toward Democracy, with Some Surprises." *The Wall Street Journal,* 28 March.

Pedersen, Lars. 1999. *Newer Islamic Movements in Western Europe.* Bookfield, VT: Ashgate Publishing.

———. 1996. "Islam in the Public Discourse in Denmark". In *Muslims in the Margin: Political Responses to the Presence of Islam in Western Europe,* edited by W. A. R. Shadid and P. S. van Konigsveld. Kampen, The Hague: Kok Pharos Publishing House.

Pope, Hugh. 2002. "For Saudi Women, Running a Business Is a Veiled Initiative." *The Wall Street Journal,* 2 January.

"Population versus Peace." 1996. *Washington Post*, 3 June.

"Post-September 11 Attitudes." 2001. Pew Research Center for People and Press, 6 December. www.people-press.org

"Pressure on Sudan." 2001. *New York Times*, 22 July.

Pugh, Deborah. 1993a. "Yemen's Oil Pipeline Runs Where Camels Trod." *Christian Science Monitor*, 19 May.

———. 1993b. "Yemen's Remarkable Elections Are a First for Arabian Peninsula." *Christian Science Monitor*, 29 April.

Quinn, Jennifer. 2002. "Spike in Hate Crimes Followed September 11." *Toronto Star*, 26 February.

Qutb, Muhammad. 1979. "The Role of Religion in Education." In *Aims and Objectives of Islamic Education*, edited by S. N. Al-Attas, 48–62. Jeddah: King Abdulaziz University.

Ramadan, Tariq. 2002. "Islam and Muslims in Europe: A Silent Revolution Toward Rediscovery." In *Muslims in the West: From Sojourners to Citizens*, edited by Yvonne Y. Haddad. New York: Oxford University Press.

Range, Peter Roxx. 1995. "Oman." *National Geographic*, May, 112–38.

Rath, Jan, Rinus Pennix, Kees Groenendijk, and Astrid Meyer. 2001. *Western Europe and Its Islam*. Leiden: Brill.

Reed, Stanley. 2001. "Can the Saudis Step on the Gas?" *Business Week*, 24 December.

Regional Surveys of the World: Africa South of the Sahara. 1995. 24th ed. London: Europa Publications.

Regional Surveys of the World: Middle East and North Africa. 1995. 41st ed. London: Europa Publications.

Reuters. 2002. "Women Given Voting Rights." *Washington Post*, 12 March.

Richberg, Keith. 2002. "Political Shocker in France." *Washington Post*, 22 April.

Roggero, Maria Adele. 2002. "Muslims in Italy." In *Muslims in the West: From Sojourners to Citizens*, edited by Yvonne Y. Haddad. New York: Oxford University Press.

Ruff, Carolyn. 1998. "Exploring Islam." *Washington Post*, 13 May.

Sachs, Susan. 2001. "Where Muslim Traditions Meet Modernity." *New York Times*, 17 December.

Saeed, Agha. 2002. "The American Muslim Paradox." In *Muslim Minorities in the West: Visible and Invisible*, edited by Yvonne Y. Haddad and Jane Smith. New York: Altamira Press.

Salah, Said. 1982. *Spoken Arabic*. Dhahran: I.P.A.

Salem, Philip A. 1995. "Arabs in America: The Crisis and the Challenge." *Al-Hewar Magazine, The Arab-American Dialogue*, July/August, 12-15.

Saloojee, Riad. 2000. "The Nature of Islam." *The Globe and Mail*, 16 January.

Samhan, Helen. 1999. "Arab Americans." *Grolier's Multimedia Encyclopedia*.

Sardar, Ziauddin. 1994. *Introducing Muhammad*. New York: Totem Books.

———. 1977. *Science, Technology, and Development in the Muslim World*. Atlantic Highlands, NJ: Humanities Press.

Saudi Arabian Information Resource. 2001. 22 September. www.saudinf.com

Schneider, Howard. 2002. "Bahrain's New King Sets Date for Vote." *Washington Post*, 15 February.

———. 2001. "Arab Nations Brutally Quash Dissidents." *Washington Post*, 7 October.

———. 1999. "Rote Schooling in Saudi Arabia Leaves Students Ill-Suited to Work." *Washington Post*, 11 June.

Shadid, W. A. R., and P. S. van Konigsveld. 1996. "Dutch Political Views on the Multicultural Society." In *Muslims in the Margin: Political Responses to the Presence of Islam in Western Europe*, edited by W. A. R. Shadid and P. S. Van Konigsveld. Kampen, The Hague: Kok Pharos Publishing House.

———, eds. 1996. *Muslims in the Margin: Political Responses to the Presence of Islam in Western Europe*. Kampen, The Hague: Kok Pharos Publishing House.

———. 1995. *Religious Freedom and the Position of Islam in Western Europe.* The Hague: Kok Pharos Publishing House.

Shaheen, Jack. 2001. *Reel Bad Arabs: How Hollywood Vilifies a People.* Northampton, MA: Interlink Publishing Group.

———. 1997. "Our Cultural Demon—The 'Ugly Arab.'" *Washington Post,* 19 August.

———. 1984. *The TV Arab.* Bowling Green, OH: Bowling Green State University Popular Press.

Shaikh, Farzana, ed. 1992. *Islam and Islamic Groups, A World Reference Guide.* Essex, UK: Longman.

Sharabi, Hisham, and Mukhtar Ani. 1977. "Impact of Class and Culture on Social Behavior: The Feudal-Bourgeois Family in Arab Society." In *Psychological Dimensions of Near Eastern Studies,* edited by L. Carl Brown and Norman Itzkowitz, 240–56. Princeton: Darwin Press.

Sheridan, Mary Beth. 2002. "Backlash Changes Form, Not Function." *Washington Post,* 4 March.

Shipler, David K. 1986. *Arab and Jew, Wounded Spirits in a Promised Land.* New York: Penguin Books.

Simonsen, Jorden Baek. 2002. "Globalization in Reverse and the Challenge of Integration: Muslims in Denmark." In *Muslims in the West,* edited by Yvonne Y. Haddad. New York: Oxford University Press.

Slade, Shelley. 1981. "The Image of the Arab in America: Analysis of a Poll of American Attitudes." *Middle East Journal* 35, no. 2 (Spring): 143–62.

Stewart, Desmond. 1972. *The Arab World*. New York: Time-Life Books.

Stowasser, Barbara Freyer. 2002. "The Turks in Germany." In *Muslims in the West: From Sojourners to Citizens*, edited by Yvonne Y. Haddad. New York: Oxford University Press.

Sunier, Thijl, and Mira van Kuijeren. 2002. "Islam in the Netherlands." In *Muslims in the West: From Sojourners to Citizens*, edited by Yvonne Y. Haddad. New York: Oxford University Press.

Telhami, Shibley. 2002. "Polling and Politics in Riyadh." *New York Times*, 3 March.

Thomas, Anthony, and Michael Deakin. 1975. *The Arab Experience*. London: Namara Publications.

Tlemcani, Rachid. 1997. "Islam in France: Myth and Reality." *The Middle East Quarterly*. Middle East Forum, March. www.meforum.org/meq

Tucker, Judith. 1991. "Women in the Arab World." *The Arab World in the Classroom*. Center for Contemporary Arab Studies, Georgetown University.

UNHCR (UN High Commission for Refugees). 2001. United Nations, 18 December. www.unhcr.ch

Vertovec, Steven. 2002. "Islamophobia and Muslim Recognition in Britain." In *Muslims in the West: From Sojourners to Citizens*, edited by Yvonne Y. Haddad. New York: Oxford University Press.

Vertovec, Steven, and Ceri Peach, eds. 1997. *Islam in Europe, The Politics of Religion and Community*. London: Macmillan.

Vick, Karl. 2001. "Sudan, Newly Helpful, Remains Wary of U.S." *Washington Post*, 10 December.

Viorst, Milton. 1991. "The House of Hashem." *New Yorker*, 7 January, 32–52.

Vogt, Kari. 2002. "Integration through Islam? Muslims in Norway." In *Muslims in the West: From Sojourners to Citizens*, edited by Yvonne Y. Haddad. New York: Oxford University Press.

Waldman, Peter. 1995. "Leap of Faith: Some Muslim Thinkers Want to Interpret Islam for Modern Times." *The Wall Street Journal*, 15 February.

Waxman, Sharon. 2001. "I Love You, Now Go Away." *Washington Post*, 17 December.

Welch, Matt. 2002. "The Politics of Dead Children." *Online Journalism Review*, March.

Wenden, Catherine Wihtol de. 1996. "Muslims in France." In *Muslims in the Margin: Political Responses to the Presence of Islam in Western Europe*, edited by W. A. R. Shadid and P. S. van Konigsveld. Kampen, The Hague: Kok Pharos Publishing House.

"Where the North Meets the South, the Pollution Charges Fly." 1993. *Christian Science Monitor*, 27 January.

Willis, David K. 1984. "The Impact of Islam." *Christian Science Monitor* (Weekly International Edition), 18–24 August.

World Development Indicators. 2001. The World Bank.

World Development Report. 2000/2001. The World Bank.

World Factbook, 2001. 2001. Washington, DC: Central Intelligence Agency and *Middle East Review*.

World Population Prospects. 1999. New York: United Nations.

Wright, Robin. 2001. "King Abdullah II." *Los Angeles Times*, 8 April.

Yousef, Fathi S. 1974. "Cross-Cultural Communication Aspects of Contrastive Behavior Patterns between North Americans and Middle Easterners." *Human Organization* 33, no. 4 (Winter): 383–87.

Zogby, John. 2001. "American Muslim Poll, November– December- 2001." Zogby International Polling/Market Research. Washington, DC. mail@zogby.com

About the Author

Margaret K. (Omar) Nydell is a widely respected scholar and professor of both Standard Arabic and many Arabic dialects. She is currently a visiting associate professor in the Department of Arabic at Georgetown University in Washington, D.C. She was an Arabic linguist for the Foreign Service Institute, U.S. Department of State, in Washington, D.C., and directed the advanced training school in Tunis, Tunisia. She has also headed several Arabic materials development projects and directed a summer Arabic program in Tangier, Morocco.

Dr. Nydell's publications include *Syrian Arabic through Video* (1995), *Introduction to Colloquial Arabic* (1993), and a six-book series *From Modern Standard Arabic to the* (regional Arabic) *Dialect*; dialects in this series include Levantine, Egyptian, Iraqi, Gulf, Moroccan, and Libyan. Many of Dr. Nydell's langugage books are in use as textbooks.

On a consulting basis, Dr. Nydell has lectured on Arabic language and conducted Arab cultural orientations sessions since 1969 for the Department of State, the Foreign Service Institute's School of Area Studies, Amideast, National Council for U.S.-Arab Relations, Booz Allen & Hamilton, Exxon-Mobil, and the Federal Bureau of Investigation.

Margaret Nydell holds a Ph.D. in Applied Linguistics with a minor in Arabic from Georgetown University and a master's degree in Arabic, also from Georgetown University. She has lived and worked in Morocco, Saudi Arabia, and Tunisia, and she completed postgraduate studies at the American University in Cairo.